Developmental Psychology and Young Children's Religious Education

Developmental Psychology and Young Children's Religious Education sets out to identify the conceptual pre-requisites for young children's religious education learning and clearly highlights the challenges that children and their teachers encounter in the RE educational process.

Based on a study with 431 children aged 5 to 7 years from different schools, faith and non-faith, and 47 teachers from the same schools as the children, this book offers an insightful look into younger children's religious education, providing statistical evidence to dismantle the belief that young children lack the ability to conceptualise God in abstract terms. The information obtained from these children and their teachers reveals a major discrepancy between the teachers' perceptions of young children's conceptual abilities for RE learning, on the one hand, and children's actual abilities revealed in their responses throughout the study, on the other. Based on the evidence described in the volume, Petrovich argues that teacher-training courses for primary RE need to be designed to include a substantial component of contemporary developmental research that is of direct relevance to children's conceptual abilities and understanding of abstract concepts.

Developmental Psychology and Young Children's Religious Education is essential reading for students and researchers in developmental psychology, religious education, teacher education, education studies and cultural anthropology.

Olivera Petrovich is a developmental psychologist in the Department of Experimental Psychology at the University of Oxford, UK. Her research deals with the development of religious understanding in children and adults from different cultures.

Developmental Psychology and Young Children's Religious Education

Olivera Petrovich

Routledge
Taylor & Francis Group
LONDON AND NEW YORK

Cover image: My First Sermon by John Everett Millais, 1863 © City of London Corporation

First published 2022
by Routledge
4 Park Square, Milton Park, Abingdon, Oxon OX14 4RN

and by Routledge
605 Third Avenue, New York, NY 10158

Routledge is an imprint of the Taylor & Francis Group, an informa business

British Library Cataloguing-in-Publication Data
A catalogue record for this book is available from the British Library

ISBN: 978-0-367-43619-3 (hbk)
ISBN: 978-0-367-43620-9 (pbk)
ISBN: 978-1-003-00463-9 (ebk)

DOI: 10.4324/9781003004639

Typeset in Times New Roman
by MPS Limited, Dehradun

Contents

List of figures vii
List of tables ix
Preface xi
Acknowledgements xiii

1 Introduction 1

2 Research design and fieldwork: Rationale and method 15

3 Children's perceptions of and attitudes to school RE: Interview findings 21

4 Everyday religious understanding: The natural-theological reasoning test 41

5 Children's concepts of God: Everyday and RE-based 59

6 Teachers' perceptions of young children's abilities for RE learning 77

7 Religious understanding in the early years: What can RE learn from young children? 91

8 Conclusion 97

References 109
Author Index 117
Subject Index 119

Figures

3.1	Percentages of children from different school denominations according to the amount of RE story recall.	23
3.2	Percentages of 5-, 6- and 7-year olds recalling RE story to the level corresponding with No recall, Limited recall and Detailed recall.	24
3.3	Percentages of children from different school denominations responding to the question whether a recalled story is about God.	25
3.4	Percentages of children from different school denominations answering the question about the meaning of religious words encountered in school RE.	27
3.5	Percentages of children from different school denominations and their attitudes to school assemblies.	31
3.6	Percentages of children from different school denominations and their judgements of RE as Both hard and easy, Hard and Easy.	33
4.1	Mean numbers of correct responses (out of six) in the four conditions of the Origin Task according to children's age.	44
4.2	Mean numbers of correct responses (out of six) in the four conditions of the Origin Task according to children's schools.	45
4.3.1	Reproduced with permission from Petrovich (2019).	46
4.4.1	Reproduced with permission from Petrovich (2019).	47
4.3	Mean numbers of correct responses (out of six) in the Animacy Task according to children's schools.	50
4.4	Mean numbers of correct responses (out of six) in the Origin and Animacy Tasks according to children's age.	51
4.5	Mean numbers of correct responses (out of six) in the Origin and Animacy Tasks according to children's schools.	51
4.6	Origin of matter: Percentages of children in each age group selecting Eternal, Created and Neither options in response to the first cosmological question.	55

4.7 Origin of matter: Percentages of children from different schools selecting Eternal, Created and Neither options in response to the first cosmological question. 55
4.8 God's role in the origin of matter: Percentages of children in each age group selecting "Matter first" and "God first" in response to the follow-up cosmological question. 56
4.9 God's role in the origin of matter: Percentages of children from different schools selecting "Matter first" and "God first" in response to the follow-up cosmological question. 57
5.1 Mean scores (out of two) on abstractness of children's Image of God, Image justification and Question about God responses according to age. 63
5.2 Mean scores (out of two) on abstractness of children's Image of God, Image justification and Question about God responses according to school denomination. 64
8.1 Millais's 1864 painting "My second sermon" © Guildhall Art Gallery (City of London Corporation). 104

Tables

3.1 Frequencies and percentages of children's RE story recall according to school denomination. 23
3.2 Frequencies and percentages of children's responses to the question about the meaning of uttered religious words according to school denomination. 27
4.1 Mean numbers of correct responses (out of six) and standard deviations (in parentheses) in the four conditions of the Origin Task according to age. 44
4.2 Mean numbers of correct responses (out of six) and standard deviations (in parentheses) in the two conditions of the Animacy Task according to age. 49
5.1 Mean scores (out of two) with standard deviations (in parentheses) on abstractness of Image of God, Image justification and Question about God responses according to age. 63
5.2 Mean scores (out of two) with standard deviations (in parentheses) on abstractness of Image of God, Image justification, and Question about God according to school denomination. 64
5.3 Frequencies and percentages (in parentheses) of children's justifications for not having a question of interest about God. 66

Preface

The current book is based on a *psychological* study designed to address those conceptual issues that are most relevant to school-based religious education (RE) of young children. Its starting point is therefore different from that of education professionals, who have published the most about RE and who bring to the subject of RE different skills and perspectives. The two disciplines – developmental psychology and primary education – are, however, closely related, as evidenced by the teachers' interviews while reflecting on their experience of teaching RE to children of primary school age. Many had stated with utmost clarity that the main difficulty facing them as primary RE teacher is not knowing how much young children can understand the material presented to them in RE lessons, especially the abstract ideas conveyed to them through that material.

The current volume is a product of my long-standing interest in young children's understanding of metaphysical concepts, notably those that are specific to religion and theology. Its aim is to document young children's endeavour to grapple with the big questions asked by philosophers and theologians yet not being taken equally seriously by those in charge of educating them. While doing research with young children I discovered that their teachers felt equally challenged by the task of educating 5- to 7-year olds in a domain so different from their other teaching but for which they had no or very little relevant training. It is thus hoped that the book may prove useful to all concerned with young children's understanding and learning of religious concepts – parents, schools, religious organisations as well as educational bodies involved in training RE teachers.

Acknowledgements

I am grateful to the following educational charities and funding organisations for their financial support to carry out the research on which this book is based: Esmée Fairbairn Foundation, Wingate Scholarships, Hockerill Educational Foundation, Culham Educational Foundation, Keswick Hall Trust, Sarum St Michael Educational Charity and The Mercers' Company. I thank the Department of Experimental Psychology at Oxford for the help and assistance received during the research. Above all, I owe gratitude to the children and teachers of the schools where the research took place for their time and enthusiasm for taking part in the project. I learned a great deal in the process. Thanks also to Penny Thompson who read the manuscript in its final stages and for her constructive and valuable feedback.

Permission to reproduce *My First Sermon* by Sir John Millais on the front cover and *My Second Sermon* in Chapter 8 also by Sir John Millais obtained with thanks to Guildhall Art Gallery © London Metropolitan Archives (City of London).

Chapter 1

Introduction

The ongoing public debate about religious education (RE) in British schools indicates that the case for its place on the curriculum is far from having been convincingly made. One of the main controversies has been its doctrinal or faith content, with an increasing emphasis on multi-faith syllabuses for all age groups, most recently affirmed in the *Religion and Worldviews Report* by the Commission on Religious Education (CoRE, 2018). Also prominent have been the arguments that religion should be taught as a branch of social studies, history, English literature, or not be included in the curriculum at all unless it also teaches atheism as one of the worldviews (e.g., *The National Secular Society Briefing Paper*, 2013). Arguments of this kind question the aims of school RE and cast doubt on its educational contribution as being any different from that made by some of the other school subjects. The main problem with this rationale, however, is that it disregards those concepts and ideas that are specific to religion and theology and thus cannot be addressed in the other domains of children's learning. Such an oversight may not be of any significance if it were based on evidence that the concepts and ideas handled by religion or theology play no role in children's cognitive development. As we shall see later in this volume, evidence from young children makes the oversight untenable. Nevertheless, because each of the views in the debate can claim some support for its position, or appears to result from valid inference, it is those elements of reasonableness that make it more difficult to dismiss the issue of school-based RE as irrelevant.[1]

Seeing that religious education (or any of its synonyms) is a compulsory school subject in many parts of the world, including British schools, and a matter of children's rights more broadly (Schweitzer, 2005), it is perplexing that no psychological research has so far purposely addressed children's cognitive potential for, and effects of, this form of learning on their development. In the current book, I focus on children of primary school age and leave out any substantial references to secondary RE for two main reasons: First, the foundational significance of this developmental period in children's education in general and, secondly, the paucity of primary RE literature, especially its lack of empirical evidence pertaining to this age range.

DOI: 10.4324/9781003004639-1

Thus, for example, even the publications that explicitly mention primary age, and acknowledge the importance of considering young children's development, do not cite any psychological research that may corroborate the claims made in those publications, not least those made about young children's conceptual abilities needed for RE (e.g., Bastide, 1992; Erricker, Lowndes & Bellchambers, 2011; Grimmitt, 2000, 2008; Kay, 2002; Kohn, 2019; McCreery, 2005; Revell, 2005). Consequently, many of the proposed conceptions of school RE are speculative, relying on RE teachers' classroom and personal experiences, on various religious groups' expectations and the like, rather than on evidence obtained from young children through systematic research of their capacity for RE learning. In view of all the above, it would be hard for a developmental psychologist to see how, without prior research evidence obtained specifically to address children's potential for grappling with different RE concepts, an appropriate RE syllabus could be designed, *pace* educationists' expectations that a syllabus agreed in a "democratic process involving religious groups, teachers and local authority representatives ... *ought* to be satisfactory" (Kay, 2002, p. 210).

Paradoxically, rather than achieving a consensus, an adult-led and adult-centred conception of primary RE has resulted in RE being widely perceived as a divisive and controversial topic. For consensus is far more likely to achieve when opinions are grounded in some relevant evidence, in this case, in research findings pertaining to children's cognitive development of direct relevance to RE, especially their conceptual abilities for RE learning and any educational benefits of RE input for their cognitive development. Without such evidence to guide and constrain conflicting adult preferences a truly educational RE is not possible.

Whilst the CoRE Report (2018) cited earlier devotes most of its content to secondary RE, it merits attention in the context of primary RE too because of its view of religion as a cultural variable, one that is concerned with beliefs and practices of diverse religious cultures and traditions rather than any particular religious concepts, notably the concept of God, as a topic of RE.[2] A cultural, rather than cognitive, framework of RE is being promoted on the grounds that it enhances children's acquisition of the skills needed for life in a multi-faith society with a special emphasis on social and emotional skills. Yet it overlooks RE's potential to equip children with cognitive skills that are valid for life in any type of society as well as for their learning in other domains. A parallel with children's education in science, maths, and literacy can be useful here because learning in those domains is likewise aimed at equipping children with skills that can be generalised to a wider variety of challenges and tasks and which are clearly conceptual. The same rationale ought to apply in the case of RE on the grounds that every aspect of children's learning should seek to make a contribution to their overall development, cognitive as well as social and emotional. Put simply, from the viewpoint of developmental psychology, RE needs to be seen as a primarily conceptual domain that involves children's reasoning about the issues inherent in religion or theology rather than just a domain of social and cultural knowledge acquisition which, indeed, can be provided by several other school subjects. Only such a change can counter the widespread perception and advocacy of RE as a vehicle of young children's social and emotional rather than cognitive development, which significantly detracts from its potential to fulfil its proper educational role.

Based on the findings obtained for this volume as well as on the extant RE literature, it is arguable that RE provision for children aged 5 to 7 years needs to overcome two major challenges: (a) scepticism regarding children's cognitive capacities needed for understanding its teaching, and (b) content of RE teacher training courses that are at present not designed to equip trainee teachers with psychological knowledge and skills needed for understanding their pupils' conceptual abilities for the subject as a precondition for their learning in it. In this book, I address mainly the former and argue that a legitimate case for RE as one of the core subjects in primary education can be most persuasively made if the cognitive-psychological reasons for such a study can be identified. As developmental research on children's learning in different domains of knowledge has consistently shown, such a rationale ensures that both children's attention and motivation to learn are engaged; for children are not passive observers and recipients of information but its active processors, who ask questions and form hypotheses about the world around them as they seek to understand its complexity. In the process of doing so, children construct veridical concepts and develop theories which enable them to make sense of what they observe. Before considering evidence obtained from children in the forthcoming chapters, a look at some of the past psychological contributions to education, specifically RE, may be useful from the viewpoint of the interdisciplinary effort that ought to involve both disciplines.

Psychology and RE: A history of the relationship

Whilst contemporary developmental psychology furnishes a very different picture of young children's abstract abilities in many areas of their learning than that found in the RE literature, the perception of RE, and religion in general, as a non-cognitive topic has a long history in psychology (e.g., Bovet, 1928; Piaget, 1928; Sully, 1903). This stance was reinforced by Goldman, who argued that "the capacity to deal with ideas of more abstract nature tends to develop during the second to third year of secondary schooling" (Goldman, 1965, p. 31). Prior to this age, according to both Piaget and Goldman, children's religious understanding is distorted by their artificialist and anthropomorphic beliefs which imply, respectively, that natural things are made by people and that God is a man. As Goldman put it, artificialism and anthropomorphism constitute the key aspects of children's religion which, in essence, is parental: "From our knowledge of the young child, we know that parents are regarded in divine terms" (Goldman, 1965, p. 51). The notion that parents provide the earliest models of deity predates Goldman's writings and is common in the psychological literature on childhood religion, most explicitly in Piaget's assertions about the origin of religion in the filial sentiment, or the child's "piety" for his parents (1928, p. 18). Piaget, however, did not study children's religious understanding but accepted Bovet's (1924) claim that young children perceive their parents as endowed with divine attributes of omnipotence, omniscience and moral perfection, a perception that vanishes once children discover their parents' limitations (at age 6 years) and start to ask about natural origins. Such discoveries are said to lead them to transfer their religious sentiment to a higher object or God. Bovet's evidence for parental religion is at best anecdotal, consisting mainly of letters written by parents about their children and of adults' recollections of their own childhood. Piaget did not question any of those claims but took them for granted and interpreted children's sporadic utterances involving God as consistent with Bovet's ideas (Petrovich, 1988a). Other writers have likewise alleged that the divine image, or concept of deity, is determined by the individual's experiences within the family and which hence corresponds with adults' descriptions of their parents as providers of our earliest experiences of transcendent power (e.g., Fowler, 1986; Heller, 1985; Hinde, 1999; Vergote et al., 1969).

Building on Piaget's (1925, 1977) theory of artificialism, Goldman argued that children's religious understanding develops through a series of stages from egocentric and concrete to abstract and called for RE to be "child-centred", that is, focused on young children's social and emotional needs rather than conceptual. Accordingly, RE teachers were advised to introduce children to religion "playfully" as opposed to rationally, in order to enable them to "fantasise their way into religion" through dance, drama and music (Goldman, 1965, p. 67). His recommendations later became known as the "implicit" approach to RE in primary school (e.g., Attfield, 1984; Cox, 1983) and its impact on RE policy-makers turned out to be, as Goldman himself put it, "very far reaching" (1965, p. 67).

Goldman's broader psychological claim is that pre-adolescent children cannot reason logically or deductively in any domain, including religious, but only in concrete images. He reached this conclusion on the basis of children's responses to the questions about the Bible from the perspective of "liberal-theological" Christianity. It is important to point out that Goldman did not employ any of the standard methodological procedures (control variables) used in psychological research to ensure that the findings did not confound children's reasoning ability, on one hand, and their factual knowledge (in this case of the Bible), on the other (Petrovich, 1988b). Without such a distinction properly maintained, it is not possible to determine what reasoning patterns in children might be universal, which

Goldman seemed to be addressing. To verify such a claim would require that children from diverse religious backgrounds and cultures should be tested under the same conditions while also taking account of children's prior familiarity with the content or material and the linguistic terms used in the testing, none of which Goldman adhered to.

Whilst Bible stories need not be an unsuitable material for investigating young children's capacity for logical and abstract reasoning, in his selection of the narratives Goldman failed to consider that the stories reporting miracles are qualitatively different from any other Biblical passages and thus less suitable for testing young children's logical capacity. To begin with, miracles are exceptional events, i.e., rare and highly irregular occurrences (Polkinghorne, 2002; Ward, 2002). As such, they need to be interpreted in accordance with certain rules and conventions that younger children are unlikely to be familiar with. Unless one is already familiar with those rules, it is not possible to account for miraculous events in terms of logical accuracy. For example, the child who said that if Moses had been deaf he could not hear God because "Deaf people don't hear" did not violate any rules of logic but only the standards of theological accuracy that Goldman employed in the test (i.e., "liberal Christianity"). Bucher's (1991) endorsement of Goldman's conclusions regarding children's understanding of parables merits similar criticisms, in addition to being based on a small sample (28 participants aged 7 to 50 years), with only a handful of those aged 7 years.

Other studies published in the 1960s and 1970s upheld Goldman's conclusions about young children's limited cognitive abilities as a major obstacle to their religious understanding (e.g., Elkind, 1964, 1966; Greer, 1972; Nye & Carlson, 1984). Although Elkind proposed a distinction between "spontaneous" and "acquired" religious concepts, he took both these categories to be dependent on cultural input. Thus, in Elkind's view, spontaneous religious concepts reflect "the spontaneous meaning children attach to their religious denomination" (1964, p. 44). "Religious denomination", however, *is* a cultural construct; one can only belong to a denomination as a result of social and cultural learning, typically by virtue of being a member of a particular cultural and social group. Put differently, people acquire concepts of themselves as being Christian, Hindu, Jewish or Muslim, through social and cultural learning from other members of the group. In contrast, spontaneous acquisition of concepts, as this term is used in post-Piagetian developmental psychology, refers to the concepts that even preverbal children acquire naturally on the basis of their everyday experience of the world (e.g., R. Gelman & Baillargeon, 1983; Wellman & S. Gelman, 1992). Whilst individuals of any age may respond in their own way ("spontaneously") to culturally derived ideas, this sense of spontaneity is secondary to the one with which humans acquire concepts of space, time, object, mind or cause, to mention but a few of the more basic or foundational concepts that very young children construct without any explicit instruction and coaching.

That Elkind's definition of spontaneity does not correspond with its meaning in contemporary developmental psychology is evident from his assertion that children's spontaneous religious thought is best elicited when they are asked questions that are "so absurd, to the adult way of thought, that one can be reasonably certain children have not been trained one way or the other regarding them" when answering questions such as, *Are all boys and girls in the world Catholic? How do you become Jewish? Can you be Protestant and American at the same time?* (1964, p. 42). Instead of searching for idiosyncrasies and peculiarities in young children's understanding of cultural ideas, as Elkind advocates, contemporary researchers of children's cognitive development look for general patterns characteristic of different age groups, i.e., similarities as well as differences across age, where all participants are tested under the same task conditions that are designed to be relevant to a particular conceptual domain. In the literature dealing with children's religious understanding, however, the "absurd questions" rationale still prevails. For example, in a study investigating children's capacity for non-literal comprehension of religious constructs, the authors asked 5 to 16 year olds to respond to questions such as: *How old is God? What does God look like? Where did God get his name? Does God get mad?* (Nye & Carlson, 1984). Even some recent developmental studies on children's religious understanding, including their concepts of God, do not overcome many of the problems discussed above but implicitly adhere to Elkind's rationale by continuing to ask children preposterous questions about God in order to uncover "spontaneous" patterns of early religious understanding (e.g., Kiessling & Perner, 2014). Even though children's responses to such questions are bound to reflect their language development and its cultural use, in practice they are often interpreted as evidence that children's concepts of God, and of the world in general, parallel Piaget's stages of cognitive development, i.e., undergo transition from concrete to abstract.

Although there has been a revival of interest in anthropomorphism in recent developmental research (e.g., Barrett, 2000; Harris & Koenig, 2006), those studies do not always manage to overcome some of the weaknesses mentioned above, most of all by failing to specify the mechanisms by which the transition from conceptualising God as a human being (i.e., one's parent) to engendering a concept of an invisible (i.e., abstract) agent occurs (Petrovich, 2019). The fact is that no psychological evidence has ever demonstrated the existence of "parental religion"; Piaget's (and Bovet's) authority seemed sufficient for those claims to remain unchallenged for too long. Thus Goldman's assertion that the most fundamental prerequisites for RE do not exist in the early years of children's education is continuous with Piaget's theory that young children's understanding of the world is radically different from that of older children and adults.

The pervasive scepticism among RE specialists regarding young children's capacity to understand an abstract concept of God was never tested or subjected to scrutiny by researchers in developmental psychology. Although a number of pertinent criticisms of Goldman's ideas were made by non-psychologists, they lacked the empirical backup (e.g., Attfield, 1984; Howkins, 1966). Howkins, for instance, accepted Goldman's judgement that children lack the ability to understand the Bible although he questioned Goldman's way of presenting its content to children, concluding that, "The idea that children are pre-religious or sub-religious before adolescence needs careful examination" (1966, p. 23). Attfield too was prepared to accept Goldman's claims about young children's inability to think in abstract terms but nevertheless argued that RE should emulate other school subjects by finding new or "better ways of introducing theological concepts to young minds" analogous to introducing to them those mathematical concepts that they find "too difficult or abstract" (1984, p. 10).

Another method that researchers have often relied on as a way of exploring young children's religious understanding is asking them to draw pictures of God. The main shortcoming of the drawing method is its implicit assumption that concepts of abstract entities, in this case of God, can somehow be represented visually without thereby grossly violating the fundamental characteristic of God, i.e., transcendence of space and time and hence invisibility. Paradoxically, researchers who used drawings as a method for eliciting children's concepts of God have done so in the belief that the method is ideally suited to this goal precisely because children can only think in terms of concrete images (e.g., Gates, 1977; Goldman, 1964; Harms, 1944; Heller, 1985; Pitts, 1977; Pnevmatikos, 2002). Pitts, for example, argued that because the child is a concrete thinker, in order to discover his or her conception of God, "what better and simpler way is there than the vehicle of pencil and paper" (p. 123). Yet, as Pitts discovered, the request to draw God "caused many a furrowed brow, gaping mouth, and expression of dismay", adding that, "Many of the younger subjects especially seemed at a loss as to where to start and what to do. Some were on the verge of tears ..." (1977, p. 127).

The use of drawings for exploring children's concepts of invisible entities may only be appropriate if a control condition exists whereby children are given the option of rejecting the notion that God can be depicted in a visual form by declining to draw a picture of God. In one small study, where 6- to 8-year-old children were given such a choice, the majority of them refused to draw God (McKelvie, 1996). It is also possible to establish, by eliciting children's justification responses, whether those who volunteer to draw God do so on the understanding that the produced drawing is a copy of a previously seen image, whether on TV, in a book, or in a place of worship rather than their own understanding of God's likeness.

To sum up thus far, an evaluation of Piaget's legacy in the developmental psychology of religion ought to convey its main limitations as a theory that aims to provide a framework for research of religious development, similar to the evaluations that have taken place in most other domains of cognitive development (e.g., biology, ethics, physics). Although rarely cited as an aspect of Piaget's broad epistemological interests, his 1920s writings on religion in adults, based in part on an exploration of religious motivation and attitude among his colleagues in Geneva, illustrate sufficiently Piaget's non-cognitivist stance towards religion. Thus, in his view, psychology of religion is an application of psychoanalysis to a person's relationships with those around him, especially in childhood; as such, psychology of religion aims to uncover the unconscious motives that "push the individual to choose immanence or transcendence, and the motives to accept or reject beliefs" (Piaget, 1928, p. 17). It is interesting that, although RE literature and most recent guidance regarding primary RE teaching no longer mention either Piaget or Goldman, its enduring conception as a domain concerned with human relationships rather than with, primarily, questions pertaining to divinity, represents a continuum with those very same psychological sources.

Contemporary developmental research and its relevance to RE

The last few decades or so have seen a flurry of publications – books, articles and newly founded journals – all offering titles classifiable as "psychology of religion". Much of this new research deals with children, more specifically, with children's "religious cognition". It is thus odd that none of the recent psychological studies on children's religious concepts has addressed school-based RE and its role in cognitive development. Instead, researchers interested in the development of religious understanding have looked at children's concepts of death, afterlife, soul and prayer in different cultures. What is important to note is that the social-cultural framework for investigating children's religious understanding is underpinned by the idea that all children's concepts associated with religion are socially and culturally transmitted rather than allowing for the possibility that some religious concepts children may acquire spontaneously, that is, as part of their everyday learning about the world through which they acquire many of their other early concepts. The distinction between the concepts that children acquire spontaneously, on the one hand, and those that they acquire formally, on the other, is well supported by developmental research (e.g., Amsel et al., 2008; Kikas, 1998; Wellman & S. Gelman, 1998). For example, psychological research of children's conceptual understanding in other school subjects, notably biology, maths and physics, has shown that children begin to construct many of the basic scientific concepts before they acquire language, enriching them later through education. Children's understanding in the religious or theological domain (i.e., RE) is an exception in that no psychological research has hitherto considered it from the viewpoint of such a distinction, that is, as an early domain of knowledge whose core concept(s) children may acquire early and spontaneously.

Highlighting the differences between the psychological, on the one hand, and educational research, on the other, is important for any changes in the field of RE to take place. One of the key differences between the two disciplines' approaches to any domain of children's education is in their respective methodologies. In contrast to the educationists' overall preference for using Piagetian clinical interview and other qualitative procedures, contemporary developmental psychologists have argued for the need to evaluate children's performance in terms of a standard provided by the average adult performance and by direct child-adult-comparisons, while taking into account any differences in their respective relevant experiences. Developmental research of children's concepts in a number of cognitive domains suggests that observed differences between children and adults are often quantitative rather than qualitative and can be attributed to the overall differences in their experience, notably linguistic, as well as other acquired knowledge rather than children's inherently different cognitive mechanisms and operations (e.g., R. Gelman, 2000).

Methodological differences in the two disciplines – developmental psychology and primary education – are determined by the nature of the questions tackled by each discipline as well as by their distinct goals. Accordingly, psychological research seeks to identify the cognitive mechanisms and processes (e.g., attention, reasoning, language) that young children rely on in different cognitive tasks. To accomplish such a goal, psychological research typically relies on testing sufficiently large samples of individual children both before and after a planned educational intervention as well as in accordance with the criteria entailed by specific research questions. Identifying the conceptual mechanisms available to young children in a particular domain ought to enable education specialists to provide children with commensurate educational challenges and thereby widen their horizons in original and authentic ways. In turn, teachers' success, or lack of it, in implementing educational interventions suggested by psychological research is in itself an important source of information to guide further psychological research. Just as some considerable fruitful collaboration between education specialists and developmental psychologists in the last few decades has made possible genuine advancement of young children's education in language and literacy, mathematics and core science subjects, the same needs to happen in RE. Yet, as mentioned earlier, the RE literature does not discuss contemporary developmental research as at all relevant to the field of RE and nor does developmental psychology touch on RE as a domain of conceptual interest to researchers studying children's cognitive development. The reasons for this apparently mutual lack of interest are multiple as well as complex, only some of which can I address in the current volume.

As we shall see in the forthcoming chapters, both children's and teachers' data imply that the existing lack of communication between developmental psychology and primary RE is no longer tenable, not least because it entails major misunderstandings involving the key protagonists in the field of RE. Drawing attention to the consequences of the virtually non-existent relationship between the two disciplines and its effects on young children's RE learning may lead to a recognition that a new approach to primary RE is possible, one that justifies its place on the curriculum as a core subject in young children's education. In the remainder of this introductory chapter, I look at the key requirements for a viable primary RE: (1) children's ability to form abstract concepts needed for participating in a meaningful school-based RE, and (2) teachers' understanding of young children's conceptual needs and abilities as a pre-requisite for enabling pupils' RE learning. In Chapters 3–6, we will consider to what extent those requirements are met.

Children's cognition: Capacity for abstract concepts

My brief review above of the representative educational and psychological literature indicates that the two disciplines – primary RE and developmental psychology – take opposing views regarding young children's abilities to handle abstract concepts. According to the majority of educationists, young children lack the abilities needed for grappling with many of the key ideas in RE, including those pertaining to God (e.g., Bastide, 1992; Erricker, Lowndes & Bellchambers, 2011; Kay, 2002; Mountain, 2005; Nye & Carlson, 1984). For example, it has been suggested that 5 to 9 year olds don't ask "what happens when we are dead" (Bastide, 1992, p. 9), that younger children lack the ability to think in more sophisticated terms (Erricker, 2011b, p. 65; Grimmitt, 2008) and that the concept of God is too abstract for children of primary age (e.g., Mountain, 2005; Wenger, 2001). Importantly, none of the authors cites any direct and purposely obtained evidence from children to corroborate such claims. When RE publications do mention psychological sources (e.g., Lowndes, 2011a), those are usually books written by eminent psychologists several decades ago (e.g., Bruner, 1977; Donaldson, 1978; Vygotsky, 1978) none of which, moreover, addresses children's religious cognition.

Starting with the assumption that Piaget's stage theory is a valid description of cognitive development, i.e., that young children are unable to understand abstract religious concepts before the age of 10 years, education specialists have argued that RE should not be about any specifically religious and/or metaphysical concepts but, instead, should include broader "topics" or "themes". Among the examples of recommended topics are "The living differences syllabus" (Erricker et al., 2011), "Life-themes approach" (Grimmitt, 2000) or "Identity formation" (Erricker et al., 2011). Some writers also suggested that children with little formal exposure to the "religious images of God" (Mountain, 2005, p. 293) or those who have little or no "religious involvement" (Wenger, 2001) necessarily end up with an idea of God that "could be unclear" and even rejected (Mountain) or fail to develop a theoretical understanding of God, i.e., as a concept used for explaining non-religious events such as natural occurrences (Wenger). To verify empirically which of the recommendations would benefit children's RE learning, it would be necessary to conduct research with children of different age groups.

Although psychology has not made a significant and direct contribution to RE, in the past few decades there have been calls for directly relevant empirical research as a basis for any decision-making about its content (e.g., Burt, 1971; Cox, 1983). For instance, based on what some RE teachers have observed in the classroom, Cox argued that young children have "basic awarenesses" (1983, p. 39) or "innate sensitivities" that underlie a distinctly "religious response to experience" (p. 41) and which can provide a starting point for primary RE. Such hints imply the need for further research. Yet, because of the lack of collaboration between developmental psychology and primary education, decision-making about children's RE continues to be made without any systematically obtained empirical evidence to support it.

Teachers' knowledge of young children's conceptual abilities and interests

Teachers' knowledge of the subject (i.e., world religions) has been in the focus of much recent RE literature as a precondition for a successful multi-faith pedagogy (CoRE, 2018). But the prior issue, namely, teachers' knowledge of young children's abilities needed to participate in and benefit from learning RE is never discussed in the CoRE Report. In other words, whilst training teachers in the subject of world faiths is seen as a non-controversial requirement, teachers' familiarity with developmental psychology is not seen as a necessary preparation for their ability to teach RE to very young children even though only such training would enable them to face the challenges posed by younger children's conceptual and linguistic development. Put simply, developmental differences between younger and older children in terms of language and social experience in general are directly relevant to their ability to learn and communicate effectively in RE. Introducing teachers to such evidence could make a significant difference to their actual practice of teaching RE to young children. By contrast, as the data obtained from teachers in the current study show, broadening PGCE training to include additional world faiths makes no contribution to the teachers' confidence when it comes to teaching RE at primary level (Chapter 6).

The mismatch between the two criteria, i.e., children's conceptual abilities, on the one hand, and teachers' awareness of those, on the other, means in practice that children are challenged by an RE that is not commensurate with their actual abilities and interests while, at the same time, teachers are challenged by demands to teach RE to young children without an adequate psychological preparation for engaging the children's existing conceptual tools in the processing of RE content. As we shall see from the evidence reported in the book, the main challenge facing young children is the lack of a meaningful connection between their existing (i.e., pre-school) religious concepts, on the one hand, and the content of their school-based RE, on the other. Their teachers are likewise hindered by an inadequate, in some cases non-existent, training in developmental psychology, which fails to convey contemporary psychological research findings of relevance to RE learning at primary age, including the training pertaining to young children's language development as a barrier to their ability to articulate their implicit understandings and uncertainties.

Religion, spirituality and worldviews

Issues relevant to children's religious understanding and primary RE are often included under the terms "spirituality" and "worldviews" as being broader and more flexible constructs than "religion", "religious experience" or specific religious concepts, notably God (Hay & Nye, 1996). For instance, based on their conversations with children aged 6 to 10 years, Hay and Nye define spirituality as a "natural dimension of human awareness" (1996, p. 8). As Nye sees it, children's spirituality is synonymous with "relational consciousness" which is said to encompass four components: relationship with the self, with others, with things, and with God (Hay & Nye, 1998, p. 113). Whilst such a broad construct that is able to encompass both religious and secular components of one's consciousness may have some advantages when used to describe children's relations with the world around them, some researchers have questioned the usefulness of definitions which lack "empirical grounding" and adequate "operationalization" (e.g., Hill et al., 2000, p. 65).

Accordingly, Spilka (in Hill et al., 2000) identifies three ways of understanding "spirituality": (1) a God-oriented spirituality; (2) a world-oriented spirituality; and (3) a humanistic (people-oriented) spirituality. Seeing, however, that "spirituality" allows for secular as well as religious content, even Spilka's (2) and (3) spiritual orientations may involve God in some way. If this is the case, the only real distinction is that between (a) religious and (b) non-religious spirituality, regardless of what other aspects of the world may also be present in a "spiritual" experience. Zinnbauer, Pargament and Scott (1999) thus seek to differentiate between religion or religious spirituality, on the one hand, and any apparently similar, yet not religious, human experiences, on the other. Their criterion in this is an explicit "association with the sacred" that defines religion or religious spirituality (p. 907), where the "sacred" includes "concepts of God, the divine, and the transcendent" (p. 907). As the authors put it, "By connecting religion with the sacred, boundaries are marked around the construct to distinguish it from other related processes (e.g., creativity, poetry, fantasy)" (Zinnbauer, Pargament & Scott, 1999, p. 908). Their view is upheld by Koenig's (2008) argument that clarity is of paramount importance when referring to religion and spirituality as synonymous terms, which can be achieved by insisting on the distinction between the religious and the secular tendencies and frameworks in any such attempts. Koenig's argument is based on the fact that the changes in the definition of "spirituality" which have occurred over time have made the need for clarity necessary. For instance, "spiritual" used to describe "the deeply religious person, but it has now expanded to include the superficially religious person" and even "the completely secular person" (Koenig, 2008, p. 349). In Koenig's words, "Unless personal beliefs are specifically religious or in some way about the transcendent or sacred, it is not obvious why they should be called spiritual" (2008, p. 353).

The importance of having clear definitions, in this case of religious spirituality as distinct from other forms of spirituality, cannot be overstated especially in the context of children's RE. In view of the considerations described above, Nye and Hay's (1996) investigation with children aged 6 to 10 years who do not mention God or the sacred when answering existential questions (e.g., *Who am I? Where do I belong? What is my purpose?*) need not be religious according to the criteria given above, simply because religious spirituality always involves some awareness of God or the transcendent, whereas "spirituality" can be either religious or secular.

As with spirituality, the term "worldviews" also raises questions regarding its scope and clarity when used as a synonym for religion and in the context of RE. In contrast to "spirituality", the term "worldview" is more frequently discussed in connection with scientific perspectives as an alternative, or additional-to-religious, view of the world that may or may not include any religious perspectives (e.g., Cooling, 2020; Gauch, 2009a, 2009b; Hannam & Biesta, 2019; Reiss, 2009; Van Der Kooij, De Ruyter & Miedema, 2017). According to developmental research, however, it is arguable that even children of pre-school age have worldviews, that is, theories about the world, which encompass both their scientific and religious concepts and views (Petrovich, 2019). Should "worldview" come to replace the terms "RE" or "religious education", the pressure to create further distinctions within its reference will undoubtedly continue in order to maintain clarity of the term's reference, i.e., as either being synonymous with religion or distinct from it.

Notes

1 In this book, I address school-based RE rather than the RE provided in the home or in the places of religious worship.

2 My search of the entire document for references to "God" produced only three returns, each being the beginning of a surname.

Chapter 2

Research design and fieldwork: Rationale and method

Given the prevailing view in the educational literature that children of primary age lack abstract concepts needed for understanding school RE, yet the absence of psychological evidence supporting such a view, in the current chapter I lay out the rationale for the research undertaken and describe the main methodological steps in obtaining the relevant evidence. I start from the position of familiarity with post-Piagetian developmental research which has documented young children's ability to form a variety of abstract concepts, including those that are fundamental to RE (for a review, see Petrovich, 2019). The existence of such psychological evidence necessitates that we account for any apparent difficulties that young children are said to have in RE learning according to much of the educational literature.

To begin with, my aim was to obtain the relevant information from each participant directly and under the same testing conditions. Such an approach contrasts with the most commonly used method in RE research, namely, ethnographic (e.g., Grimmitt, 2000; Jackson & Starkings, 1990; Stern, 2018), which typically involves groups of children observed in some activity or discussion ("participant observation"). The majority of ethnographic studies carried out in RE research include children older than primary school age and whose language is sufficiently developed to allow them to engage in discussion with the other research participants. Whilst ethnographic method can be useful in allowing researchers to gain some insight into the breadth of potentially relevant issues, such an approach is less suitable when it comes to the younger children who typically lack a sufficiently rich vocabulary to elaborate the nuances of their understandings and who thus require a more targeted approach designed to elicit the information needed for addressing specific issues. A further relevant point is that ethnographic approaches work well with smaller samples, when researchers can make detailed descriptions of their observations. In psychological research, however, methods are needed for analysing data from large samples of participants; in those situations quantitative analyses are more suitable for providing meaningful summaries of the vast amounts of data whilst not refraining from using qualitative methods when appropriate such as in

DOI: 10.4324/9781003004639-2

interviews. Accordingly, given the age of children in the current study (5, 6 and 7 years), and their total number (431), psychological methods and procedures were required for analysing data as they permit multiple cross-group comparisons on the different variables included in the research.

The research reported in the current volume was designed to identify some of the conceptual pre-requisites for RE that may be available to young children when they first start school as well as the challenges that children and their teachers encounter in the RE educational process. For this reason, I sought information from both children and their teachers regarding each side's experiences of participating in primary RE. Seeing that the aim of the project was to address primarily the psychological, i.e., conceptual, issues in RE learning, it was important to include several control variables. First, children from different religious backgrounds (i.e., faith schools) were recruited in approximately equal numbers across age, sex and faith as well as children of the same age range from a non-faith school. In total, children from thirteen schools in England took part in the study. Secondly, children's teachers (i.e., from the same schools as the children) were recruited to furnish their perceptions of young children's RE learning. Including the children's teachers ensures that both sides can contribute to elucidating the nature of some of the recurrent difficulties reported in the primary RE literature and thereby facilitate a better understanding and interpretation of each side's perceptions of RE in primary school. Both groups of research participants (i.e., children and teachers) were willing respondents and contributed a wealth of data directly relevant to the aims of the project.

Children provided data on two occasions: (1) RE interview session, during which each child was asked about their perception of and attitudes to different aspects of school RE, and (2) the natural-theological reasoning test, which taps into children's everyday understanding of the world as a context for emerging religious concepts. The two sessions took place at least one week apart but always in that order. Children were tested individually in a quiet space within their schools and their responses were recorded on the test sheets prepared in advance as well as tape recorded to ensure accurate transcribing of their verbatim responses.

In the RE interview children from all the participating schools and age groups were asked the same questions and under the same testing conditions, i.e., with no other child or adult being present. Children were interviewed about a set of issues bearing on the matter of their understanding of RE as a school subject, namely: (a) *memory and comprehension of RE content* (stories and religious words); (b) perception of, and attitudes to, school *assemblies*; and (c) judgements about whether RE learning is *easy or hard* and the reasons given for those judgements. Data obtained in RE interviews are reported and discussed in Chapter 3. At the end of the interview, children were also asked to say if there was anything about God that they would really like to find out, i.e., state their *own questions about God* which they had identified as being of greatest interest to them. Those data are reported and discussed in Chapter 5.

In the second session, which took place at a later date, children's everyday or untutored religious understanding was assessed by means of a picture test consisting of realistic representations (photographs) of different natural and artificial objects. Children received a number of factual questions about the objects' characteristics and mechanisms of origin (antecedent-derived origin) as well as speculative questions about the origins of unseen natural objects (primary origin). The test was developed for use with both children and adults as a way of assessing their potential to infer a concept of God in the context of everyday world, most notably when seeking to understand it in causal terms (Petrovich, 1999, 2019). The advantage of the natural-theological reasoning test is in yielding quantifiable and directly comparable data obtained from children of different religious and cultural backgrounds regarding their (a) knowledge about the physical world and its causal mechanisms; (b) ability to reflect on the world in a manner that is characteristic of most religious traditions (i.e., speculate about causal origins of natural kinds, including answering the cosmological question which asks about the beginning of the world and primary matter); and (c) abstractness of their everyday concepts of God. Data obtained in the natural-theological reasoning test are reported and discussed in Chapter 4.

In short, the aim of the natural-theological reasoning test in the current study was twofold: First, to elicit children's responses about God in the context of their reasoning about the physical world, which would allow comparisons with their concepts of God in the context of RE teaching, as probed in the RE interview (i.e., consistency between the two sets of data). The second aim of the natural-theological reasoning test was to replicate the previously obtained findings with children of pre-school age from Britain and Japan whose concepts of God as abstract or concrete were investigated by the same test (Petrovich, 2019). Children's concepts of God elicited during each testing procedure (RE interview and natural-theological reasoning test) are reported and discussed from the viewpoint of their abstractness and their role in children's religious understanding (Chapter 5).

In all, 431 children aged 5, 6 and 7 years from different faith (Anglican, Evangelical, Roman Catholic, Hindu, Jewish, Muslim) and non-faith school denominations took part. Of this number, 400 children completed both sessions of the investigation (i.e., RE interview and natural-theological reasoning test) whereas 31 children completed the RE interview but were not available for the natural-theological reasoning test due to the intervening vacation breaks that also took some of them to a higher age group.

Following the completion of the children's sessions, teachers from the same schools (*N* = 47) were interviewed about several aspects of their experience of teaching RE to young children. The inclusion of children's RE teachers was crucial for testing my overall hypothesis that some of the controversy surrounding the role of primary RE in children's cognitive development might be a consequence of a major misunderstanding regarding young children's capacity for handling abstract concepts reported in developmental literature, on one hand, and the RE teachers' expectations of young children abilities for abstract reasoning implied by the prescribed syllabus content, on the other. The aim of the questions put to the teachers was therefore to obtain their views about (a) children's capacity to comprehend abstract concepts, notably God, and participate in the different aspects of school RE, (b) usefulness of their own training for the task of teaching RE to children of primary age, and (c) what the teachers saw as the main purpose of primary RE. It was gratifying to learn from the teachers that the issues addressed in the project were seen by the teachers as vital to their ability to relate to young children's understanding of school RE. Data obtained from 47 teachers of primary RE are reported and discussed in Chapter 6.

It is important to reiterate that recruiting participants from different faith schools was a control measure needed to assist in data interpretation rather than a deliberate strategy to investigate the impact of specific religious teachings on children's responses in the study. In other words, the rationale for selecting participants from different faith backgrounds was to determine whether children from different schools and religious traditions respond in a similar or different pattern to the tests and questions used across the study. Accordingly, any similarities shown in the natural-theological reasoning test would suggest that children of the same age process the same information about the physical world in similar ways regardless of their religious background. This expectation is grounded in the fact that the questions in the test rely solely on children's everyday familiarity with the physical world around them and do not presuppose any prior RE input nor even a substantial religious vocabulary.

There has been no other comparable research design that seeks to address the place of RE in young children's cognitive development and early education or which has investigated the same issues as those tackled in the current study. Whilst a small number of studies do include both children and teachers (e.g., DeRoos, Iedema & Miedema, 2001; Miller & McKenna, 2011; Rymarz & Belmonte, 2020), differences among those studies preclude any direct comparisons with the findings of the current project. Thus, for example, although Miller and McKenna also approached school RE by seeking the views from both pupils and teachers, their sample consisted of only 27 pupils and 10 teachers and the children were significantly older (15 to 16 years old) than the children in the current study. Further, the researchers used questionnaires to elicit responses from the participants rather than interviews, as in the current study. It should also be said that Miller and McKenna's data pertaining to RE form only a part of a broader project that investigates religion as a way of promoting community cohesion equalities in schools ("Religion in education: A contribution to the dialogue or a factor of conflict in transforming societies of European countries?") which was conducted in one school only.

Nor is Rymarz and Belmonte's (2020) study of Catholic children's questions raised in RE classes comparable to the design of the current study. The authors' main interest in the study is in the pupils' acquisition of their "religious identity" (p. 121) rather than their concepts of God. As well as this, Rymarz and Belmonte did not interview children directly but sought information about them from adults, i.e., from 11 RE coordinators and 77 members of the "focus groups of experienced teachers" who work with infant, primary and secondary students (p. 120).

Finally, in a study that included 165 pre-school children, 16 teachers and 107 parents, DeRoos, Iedema and Miedema (2001) looked at individual differences in children's God concepts that are attributable to the influences by children's parents and by their teachers. In contrast, the study described in the current book asks how children from different faith and non-faith backgrounds conceptualise God in their everyday understanding of the world, on the one hand, and in the context of school RE, on the other.

Chapter 3

Children's perceptions of and attitudes to school RE: Interview findings

The current chapter describes the findings obtained from children in the RE interview according to the main issues addressed: (1) memory and comprehension of RE content (stories and religious words); (2) participation in school assemblies; and (3) judgements about whether RE learning is easy or hard and the reasons for those judgements. As mentioned earlier, the aim of the RE interview was to obtain children's perspective on school-based RE by asking them to reflect on its several aspects with a view to answering the main research question in the study, namely, whether children of primary school age construe RE lessons as being about God and, also, what connection, if any, young children make between school RE, on the one hand, and their everyday, or informal, understanding of God, on the other. The latter part of this question will be considered in Chapter 4.

Interview procedure. Children were interviewed individually in a quiet room or secluded space within their schools. The interviews were tape-recorded for subsequent verbatim transcription while notes by hand were also taken on sheets of paper containing the interview questions and the basic demographic information about each participant. All children received interview questions in the same order but minor departures from the planned sequence occurred when the need arose to resolve any ambiguities and/or possible misunderstandings. Interview data were analysed according to children's age, sex and school denomination,[1] in order to identify any similarities and differences across those variables.

The interviews began by asking each child what they did "in religious education [or RE] today or last time". It was somewhat surprising that the majority of children in the study (i.e., above 80%) were unfamiliar with the terms "religious education" and "RE" but only responded when asked whether they were "learning about God". There was some variation across the schools, however, in that some schools use alternative, faith-specific, terms for referring to RE, with which the children were familiar; for instance, in Jewish and Muslim schools children used the terms Kodesh[2] and Deen,[3] respectively, while those in Evangelical schools stated that they had Biblical studies. Although children from Hindu tradition were rather more

DOI: 10.4324/9781003004639-3

familiar with "religious education", and virtually all knew the meaning of "RE", they too, like other children, often mentioned non-RE topics and activities as part of RE. Needless to point out, children of this age do not know the meaning of "religion" either, even when stating that RE means "learning about religion". Thus, when asked what "religion" meant, one child replied "I think it means a long time ago" (age 6). When conducting interviews with the children's teachers I asked them to comment on children's lack of familiarity with the terms "religious education" and "RE", and those data will be reported in Chapter 6.

Memory and comprehension of RE content: Stories and religious words

RE stories

Following a brief introduction about the purpose of my visit to the school, I asked each child to recall a story that they had most recently listened to or read in RE. The questions of interest in this part of the study were (a) whether children aged 5–7 years can recall the gist of a selected story, and (b) whether they understood the story to be about God. Three levels of story recall were scored: (0) No recall; (1) Limited or sketchy outline, often just its theme; and (2) Detailed recall.[4] As for children's understanding of the story's religious relevance, i.e., whether it is about God, which was asked of those children who had recalled a story, their responses were scored as (0) Doesn't know, (1) No (i.e., story is not about God), and (2) Yes (i.e., story is about God).

In data analysis, I first looked at whether children from the different Christian schools (total 214) could be treated as a single group. This was not the case because of several statistically significant differences that emerged among different Christian groups; accordingly, six faith school groups (three Christian, three other faiths) and one non-faith were treated as separate school denominations. All quantitative analyses in this part of the study were carried out by Chi-square tests for independence and reported as statistically significant or not. In addition to numerical results, children's verbatim responses, selected for being representative of the variety of their response categories, are also included.

Of the 431 children in the whole study, 421 responded to the first interview question, i.e., to recall a RE story. Significant differences in the amount of children's story recall were found in relation to their school denomination, X^2 (12, N = 421) = 66.30, p = .000, Cramer's V = .28. Frequencies and percentages of the three recall levels among children from all seven types of school are displayed in Table 3.1, which shows that the majority of children in the study recalled a story in a limited or sketchy manner (48.7%), followed by those who did not recall anything (34.2%), with only 17.1% of children being able to recall a story in some detail.

Table 3.1 Frequencies and percentages of children's RE story recall according to school denomination

School	*No Recall*	*Limited Recall*	*Detailed Recall*	*Total*
Anglican	27 (30.0%)	51 (56.7%)	12 (13.3%)	90
Evangelical	8 (14.3%)	40 (71.4%)	8 (14.3%)	56
Catholic	28 (45.9%)	31 (50.8%)	2 (3.3%)	61
Hindu	14 (24.1%)	21 (36.2%)	23 (39.7%)	58
Jewish	17 (26.6%)	32 (50.0%)	15 (23.4%)	64
Muslim	32 (50.0%)	23 (35.9%)	9 (14.1%)	64
Non-faith	18 (64.3%)	7 (25.0%)	3 (10.7%)	28
Total	144 (34.2%)	205 (48.7%)	72 (17.1%)	421

Put differently, 82.9% of the total sample either did not recall anything or did so to a very limited degree. Figure 3.1 additionally shows that among "detailed recallers" the highest percentage is represented by Hindu children (39.7%), whereas zero recall scores were most frequent among children from non-faith (64.3%) and Muslim schools (50.0%). It is pertinent to point out that children from those two types of school produced low recall for different reasons. Whilst non-faith schoolchildren receive a markedly reduced input of RE stories compared to the children from faith schools, and thus

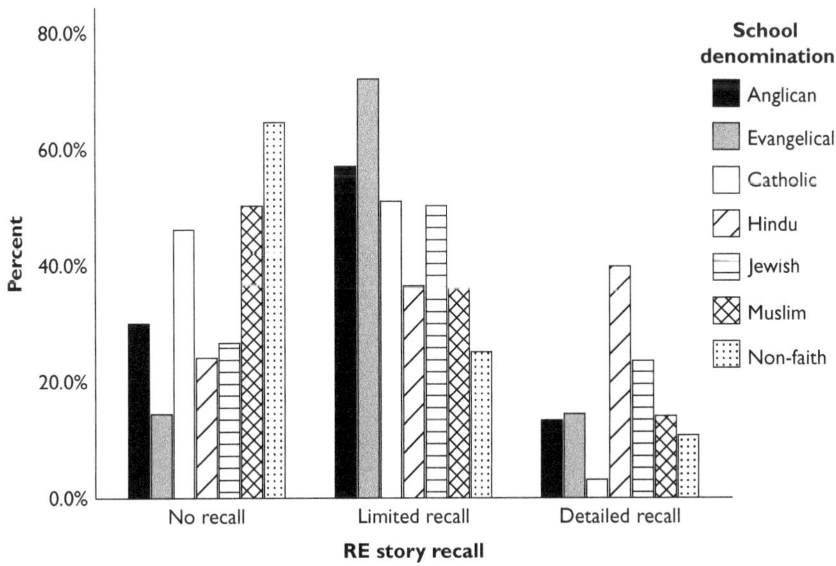

Figure 3.1 Percentages of children from different school denominations according to the amount of RE story recall.

often recall stories with non-religious content, Muslim children's poor recall rate is largely due to their limited knowledge of English when they first start formal education.

In addition to school denomination, children's age also contributed to how much they could recall: X^2 (4, N = 421) = 26.63, p = .000, Cramer's V = .18. As Figure 3.2 shows, children's ability to recall a story in detail increases with age and, conversely, failure to recall anything declines with age, a pattern that is consistent with young children's developing linguistic as well as memory skills (Mandler, 1990). In contrast, tendency to produce a limited or sketchy recall appears to be constant across all three age groups, with 6-year olds producing all three levels of recall to a similar degree. There was no significant difference between boys and girls regarding their ability to remember a story, X^2 (2, N = 421) = 4.47, p = .107.

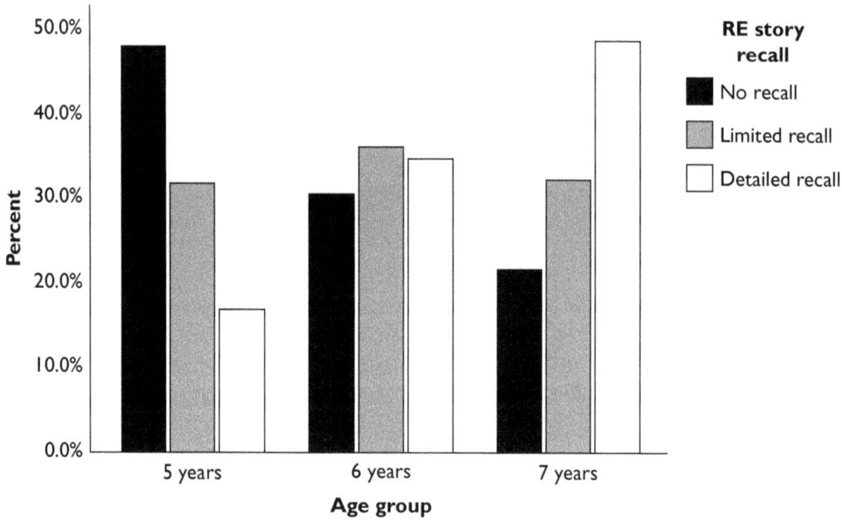

Figure 3.2 Percentages of 5-, 6- and 7-year olds recalling RE story to the level corresponding with No recall, Limited recall and Detailed recall.

When it comes to children's understanding whether a recalled story is *about God*, the majority (47.0%) affirmed that it is, 35.3% did not know, and 17.7% denied that a recalled story is about God. Statistical analysis confirmed that the differences among children from different school denominations were significant, X^2 (12, N = 249) = 26.93, p = .008, Cramer's V = .23. As Figure 3.3 illustrates, the highest percentage of children who state that the recalled story is about God, and explain in what way, are from Jewish (62. 5%), Anglican (59.0%) and Evangelical (57.5%) schools.

Figure 3.3 Percentages of children from different school denominations responding to the question whether a recalled story is about God.

The next largest category of response, *Doesn't Know*, indicates that children from Catholic (48.1%), Muslim (46.4%) and Hindu (41.9%) schools most often could not tell if the story is about God, albeit for different reasons. For example, for many Catholic children Jesus and God do not always seem to have the same reference (e.g., a recalled story is about Jesus, not about God); in the case of Hindu children, who typically mention diverse gods in the recalled stories yet deny that the recalled stories are about God, it seems that those children differentiate between "gods" and "God". This possibility is supported by the same children's data in the natural-theological reasoning test described in Chapter 4, where they consistently refer to "God" rather than "gods" when explaining the origins of natural objects. Data pertaining to children's concepts of God (Chapter 5) additionally support such an interpretation in the case of Hindu children. As for Muslim children's low scores when answering the question whether a recalled RE story is about God, the previously suggested explanation in terms of the younger children's limited knowledge of English remains appropriate seeing that for many of them English is not their first language.

In contrast to children's story recall, their understanding whether a recalled story is about God was not significantly influenced by their age, X^2 (4, N = 249) = 6.09, p = .193, although there is an upward trend with age to recognise the connection. It should be noted, however, that whilst the amount of recall may be relatively easily determined, children's responses to the question whether a recalled story is about God can be harder to disambiguate. Thus, for example, it is not always clear from children's limited recall whether the remembered story is entirely a morality tale or one where God was explicitly mentioned.

While the two sexes were similar in how much they were able to recall a story, a difference emerged in their understanding of whether or not a recalled story is about God, X^2 (2, N = 249) = 7.48, p = .024, Cramer's V = .17, in that more boys (55.6%) than girls (39.4%) said that the story was about God and, conversely, 42.2% of girls and 27.4% boys did not know if the story was about God. There is no obvious explanation for this sex difference and, generally speaking, sex differences in cognition can be difficult to interpret because they often interact with other variables.

In summary, although the majority of children maintain that they enjoy listening to stories, not all of them can recall a story even in a skeletal form. The most common first response following the request to recall a story is "I can't remember", and only with further encouragement were 5- to 7-year-old children able to recall some content and often only in a brief outline. Of those who could recall a story even briefly, 53.0% either did not know if the story was about God or denied that it was.

Religious words

Another way of assessing children's understanding of RE content is asking them to recall a prayer from RE lessons or school assemblies and question them about the meaning of its words. Virtually all of the 371 children who provided data in this part of the interview were able to recite a short prayer or chant in Arabic, Gujarati, Hebrew, Hindi or Sanskrit and, in the Christian schools, a prayer ending with *Amen*, upon which I asked each child what the words that they had uttered in the prayers meant in English. Responses were scored as (0) Doesn't Know; (1) Guessing (i.e., wrong); and (2) Understanding (i.e., correct). Children's responses in this part of the study differed significantly across the school denominations: X^2 (12, N = 371) = 111.30, p = .000, Cramer's V = .39. The frequencies and percentages of children's responses about the meaning of uttered religious words are shown in Table 3.2 and also illustrated in Figure 3.4 shown below. These data indicate that the largest category of response about the meaning of religious words encountered in school RE is Doesn't Know (62.0%), followed by Guessing (25.5%), with only 12.5% of the responses that could be categorised as Understanding, i.e., knowing the meaning of the religious words that the children had reproduced in the interview. Children from non-Christian faith schools were most unfamiliar with the meaning of the words used in school prayers, with 86% Muslim, 81.3% Jewish and 76% Hindu pupils not knowing the meaning of the uttered words. A number of them, however, were familiar with the meaning of very short prayers, notably those used in praising or thanking God.

Table 3.2 Frequencies and percentages of children's responses to the question about the meaning of uttered religious words according to school denomination

School	*Doesn't Know*	*Guessing*	*Understanding*	*Total*
Anglican	25 (42.4%)	28 (47.5%)	6 (10.2%)	59
Evangelical	19 (33.9%)	16 (28.6%)	21 (37.2%)	56
Catholic	31 (52.5%)	28 (47.5%)	0 (0.0%)	59
Hindu	38 (76.0%)	6 (12.0%)	6 (12.0%)	50
Jewish	52 (81.3%)	1 (1.6%)	11 (17.2%)	64
Muslim	49 (86.0%)	7 (12.3%)	1 (1.8%)	57
Non-faith	16 (61.5%)	9 (34.6%)	1 (3.8%)	26
Total	230 (62.0%)	95 (25.5%)	46 (12.5%)	371

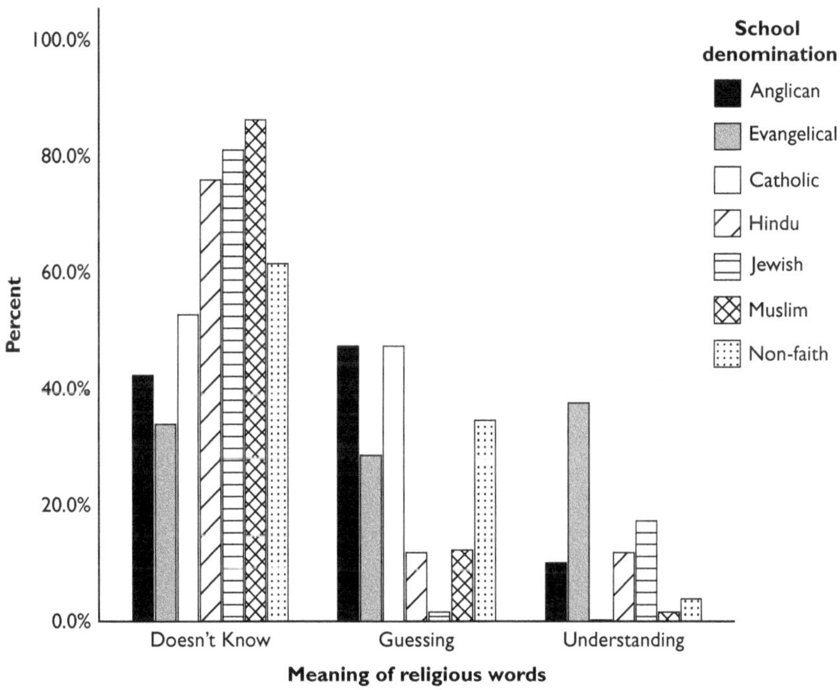

Figure 3.4 Percentages of children from different school denominations answering the question about the meaning of religious words encountered in school RE.

Whilst there is a reliable – and predictable – upward trend with age in understanding the meaning of religious words and, conversely, a decline in ignorance, these trends were not found to be significantly influenced by children's age, X^2 (4, N = 371) = 7.67, p = .104. Nor did children's sex contribute significantly to the results, X^2 (2, N = 371) = .947, p = .623. The greatest frequency of response among both sexes is in the category Doesn't Know (60.5% girls and 63.4% boys), followed by an almost identical percentage of boys and girls responding by Guessing (25.8% versus 24.4%, respectively), with a mere 14.1% of girls and 10.8% of boys evincing an understanding of the meaning of used religious words. Below is a selection of children's verbatim responses to the question about the meaning of the words used in prayers in the Doesn't Know category.

Children's statements

- I don't know what that means but that's my prayer (age 5).
- It means it's time to pray (age 5).
- I think it means to pray to God (age 5).
- Gujarati is our language to God (age 6).
- Well, all I know is "Thank you, God, and we pray" (age 6).
- The meaning in English is that you have to pray a lot, five times (age 6).
- I don't know because they haven't told us most of them … they haven't told us the meaning (age 7).
- Thank you for … it's about the morning when you wake up but I'm not very sure (age 7).
- I don't want to know what they mean … I just don't like them (age 7).

Surprisingly, when I asked the children whether they were bothered by not understanding the words that they were using, the vast majority of them and across all the schools said that they were not (e.g., "As long as God understands me, I don't really mind", age 7), and some even said that they liked it that way. While manifestly at odds with the tenets of cognitive-developmental theories, according to which understanding the meaning is a precondition for acquiring its linguistic label and retaining it in memory, and also with the evidence in the current study that children's memory for stories is hindered by not understanding their meaning (see Section 3 in this chapter), children's acceptance of uncertainty regarding the meaning of religious words used in prayer appears consistent with the notion that having a separate language for worship (e.g., liturgical) need not be an obstacle to worship but may even facilitate it. Further research would be needed before verifying such hints as reliable pointers regarding any practical recommendations.

Children from the schools whose RE is entirely in English (i.e., Christian and non-faith), and who were thus asked about the meaning of *Amen,* were also largely unfamiliar with its meaning: 45.5% said that they did not know (e.g., "I don't know, we just say it", age 7), 40.5% resorted to guessing about its meaning (see examples below), whilst only 14.0% were correct, stating that *Amen* signifies one's agreement with the prayer. The biggest difference between the children who receive RE entirely in English and those from the other faiths (i.e., whose RE includes languages other than English) is in the category Guessing, where 40.5% of those receiving RE in English, versus 8.2% of those from other faiths, resorted to guessing about the meaning of *Amen* and other religious words, respectively.

Children's attempts to make sense of the word that they use almost daily in their school prayers, i.e., *Amen*, are of interest on account of their ingenuity. By far the most common conjecture among all age groups was that *Amen* signifies the end of prayer:

- Nearly finished (age 5).
- It means it's the end of the prayer. You can't keep carrying on (age 5).

This was followed by "Thank you" conjectures (for a variety of reasons), while also frequent were the conjectures arising from associations by sound with the word "men". Examples of these and children's other creative ideas regarding the meaning of *Amen* are shown below.

- May be it means you are sending it to God (age 5).
- Well, that means God (age 5).
- Hm ... about Jesus (age 5).
- To keep God safe (age 5).
- To be good (age 5).
- It means, I think, French. [What?] God of flowers (age 5).
- It means "thank you" ... Was I right? (age 5).
- It means ... it means ... thank you (age 6).
- Amen means "thank you, and we are gonna to stop praying" (age 6).
- It means "thank you for listening to our prayer" (age 7).
- Mens means people ... Mens is the same word as people (age 5).
- We thank you, God, for all men (age 6).
- I think it means the soldiers (age 6).
- I think it's something to do with Jesus, like "a man" or something (age 7).
- It means that for the stuff we've got, we thank our men (age 7).
- All the people who got the food (age 7).
- That means "good bye" to all the dead people who have been made angels (age 6).
- I think it's "Glory to God", 'cause the angels sing it in their song so it's got to be something like "Glory to God" (age 6).
- It means "I believe" (age 7).
- I like you, God (age 7).
- It means we have to look after each other (age 7).

Before proceeding to the next section, I should point out that in this volume I do not address the broader question of young children's understanding of prayer as an activity involving God simply because little developmental research exists on this topic. Whilst the older studies relied on the methods that do not do justice to this important issue, contemporary developmental research has turned to rather different questions regarding young children's notions of prayer.[5] As an example of the older methodological approaches is a study by Long, Elkind and Spilka (1967) who undertook to investigate young children's "conception of prayer", i.e., whether prayer is connected with God, by asking children a series of questions that do not, however, mention God (e.g., *Do dogs and cats pray? What is prayer? Can you pray for more than one thing? What must you do if your prayer is (is not) answered?*). Although two (out of 20) 5-year olds did mention God in their responses, which implies that children of this age can associate prayer with God, the authors concluded that 5- to 7-year-olds only have "a dim awareness that prayers were somehow linked with the term God" (p. 104). To know at what point in their development children begin to understand prayer as involving God rather than any other agent to whom requests can be addressed is, indeed, a key question in this area of religious development and one that merits a greater research effort in the future.

School assemblies: Children's likes and dislikes

Given that school assemblies play an important role in school RE, I asked each child whether or not they enjoyed the time spent in assemblies and what their reasons were. Although the percentage of children from all the schools who like assemblies (78.6%) significantly exceeds the percentage of those who do not (9.8%), as well as those who have mixed feelings about school assemblies, i.e., both like and dislike them (11.6%), some differences among children from different schools who like assemblies were found to be statistically significant: X^2 (12, N = 397) = 42.17, p = .000, Cramer's V = .23. As Figure 3.5 shows, children from Anglican (66.3%) and Jewish (61.5%) schools seem to like their assemblies to a lesser degree than those from Evangelical (96.4%), Catholic (86.7), Muslim (86.0%) and Hindu 85.0%) schools. Children's attitudes to school assemblies should, however, be interpreted in conjunction with their justifications (i.e., reasons) for those attitudes (see examples below).

Given that 73.1% of non-faith schoolchildren also like assemblies, and that the majority of children in the study describe RE as hard (see "Judgements about RE learning as easy or hard" section), it seems that children's reasons for enjoying assemblies need not be RE related. Indeed, 5- to 7-year-olds from across the schools most often mention activities such as singing, celebrating religious festivals, their own birthdays, or receiving awards for personal achievements as the main reasons for enjoying school assemblies. Those who do not enjoy assemblies most often cite boredom due to long duration, lack of direct involvement, physical discomfort, and the

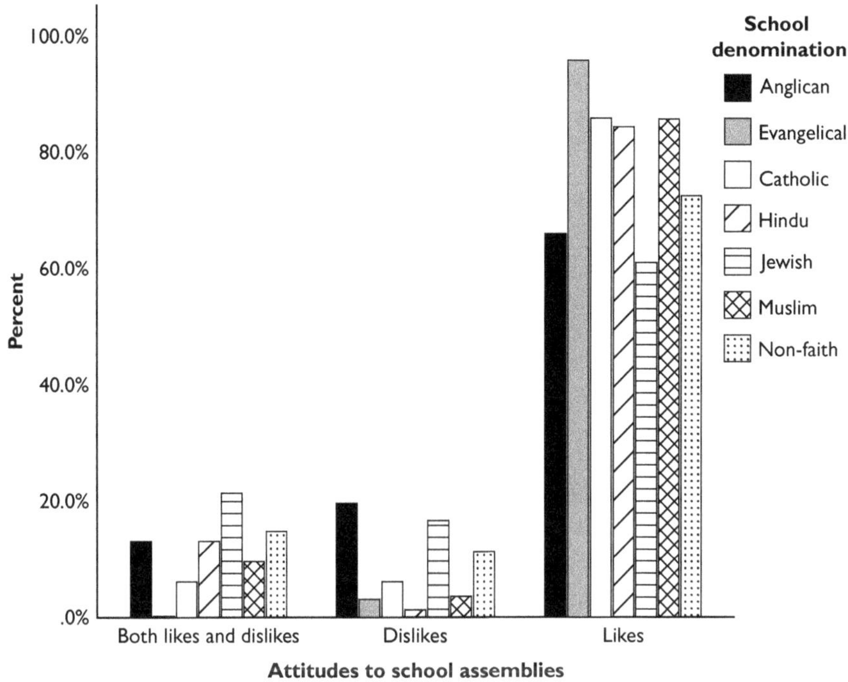

Figure 3.5 Percentages of children from different school denominations and their attitudes to school assemblies.

like, as grounds for their negative perceptions. There were no significant differences in children's attitudes to school assemblies according to age, X^2 (4, N = 397) = 8.47, p = .076, although, on the whole, younger children tend to perceive assemblies as more enjoyable than older children do. Whilst children of both sexes clearly like their school assemblies, one sex difference emerged regarding Dislikes, whereby a greater percentage of boys (13.9%) than girls (5.6%) expressed a dislike, X^2 (2, N = 397) = 8.70, p = .013, Cramer's V = .15. To repeat my earlier caveat, sex differences in cognition are not straightforward to account for as they often interact with other variables. Below are included some of the examples of children's reasons for their *likes* and *dislikes* of school assemblies.

Children's statements

- I do like assemblies but I don't like to sit down for a long time (age 5).
- I don't like davening [prayer] (age 5).
- It's boring. If we had food and snacks it would be good (age 5).

- So boring ... All you can do is stand and listen to a story (age 6).
- Not the long ones ... When I need the toilet I can't go (age 6).
- I don't like the stories but I do like singing. Stories are boring (age 6).
- Boring ... You just sit there and listen to the stuff that you already know (age 7).
- [dislikes] Singing, because it's hard to remember words for each song (age 7).
- You just have to sit down and listen ... anyway, I don't understand (age 7).

In a few instances, children expressed somewhat stronger views about their participation in school assemblies by describing them as "Really long and boring [stories] and the teachers lied to us; they said it was going to be short but it was actually very long" (age 6) or by simply stating, "I hate them" (age 7). Whilst children's justifications for their Likes and Dislikes responses provide a valuable feedback as such, in order to understand children's attitudes to school assemblies more fully it is also important to consider other relevant information, most notably children's concepts of God (Chapter 5).

Judgements about RE learning as easy or hard

The findings about children's experience of school RE described so far show that 5- to 7-year olds encounter a number of difficulties when processing RE content. To gain some insight into whether such experiences lead children to perceive RE as hard, I asked them to make easy/hard judgements about RE and state why it is so for them. The majority of children in the study (42.3%) view RE as hard, 31.2% describe it as easy, whilst 26.5% find it to be both easy and hard, i.e., some aspects easy and some hard. Children's judgements of RE as Easy, Hard or Both easy and hard differed significantly according to their school denomination, X^2 (12, N = 381) = 37.73, p = .000, Cramer's V = .22. As Figure 3.6 indicates, children from Anglican schools most often describe RE as "hard" (66.7%), whereas among those who find RE to be easy, the majority are Catholic respondents (45.9%). Children from non-faith (44.4%) and Jewish (39.7%) schools often expressed mixed feelings about the subject, describing it as both easy and hard.

Children's justifications (reasons) for perceiving RE as either easy or hard are provided below and show that their reasons for perceiving RE as hard are wide-ranging, encompassing their perceived lack of sensory and motor skills (e.g., drawing, writing letters) as well as cognitive demands and moral concerns. Whilst the use of Arabic, Hebrew and Gujarati or Sanskrit is the most commonly cited reason among children from non-Christian faith schools for perceiving RE as being hard (cf. Kohn, 2019), children from all the schools in the study frequently mentioned demands to memorise, produce drawings on RE themes ("colouring is easier"), write sentences

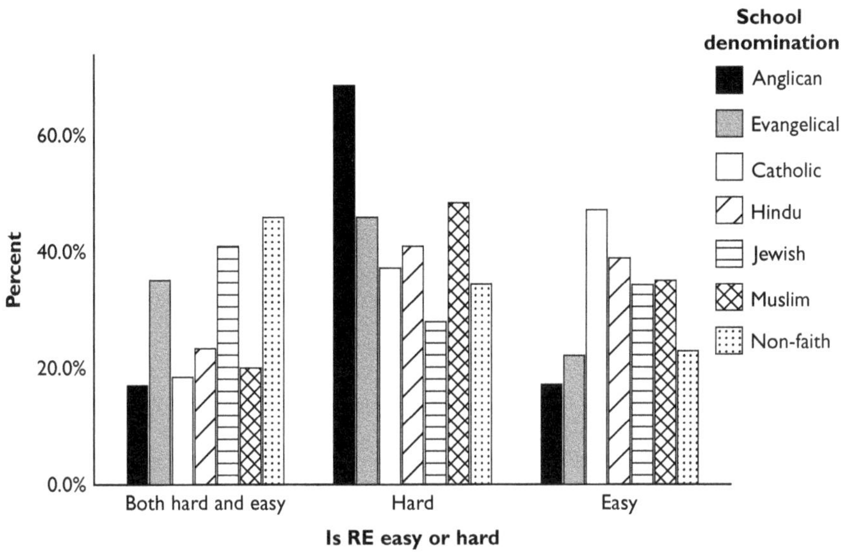

Figure 3.6 Percentages of children from different school denominations and their judgements of RE as Both hard and easy, Hard and Easy.

about RE themes as being equally hard to fulfil. Not being able to understand much of the RE content, however, emerged as the most salient among children's concerns when it comes to perceiving RE to be hard. Indeed, children from all school denominations put the greatest emphasis on their lack of understanding of the material encountered in RE lessons as the main reason for finding the subject to be hard.

Children's age too was a significant factor in their judgements whether RE is easy or hard, X^2 (4, N = 381) = 15.00, p = .005, Cramer's V = .14. The effect of age accounts for the majority of 5-year olds judging RE to be easy (46.3%). The perception of RE as an easy subject declines with age, however, and children increasingly begin to view it as either hard or both easy and hard. With age, children also become better able to identify the specific aspects of RE that are "easy" and those that are "hard", an ability that depends on their growing language proficiency. Sex differences were of marginal significance in children's judgements of RE as easy or hard, X^2 (2, N = 381) = 5.97, p = .051, with a somewhat greater frequency of Easy responses among boys (36.5%) than among girls (25.9%).

Seeing that by far the most common among children's reasons for perceiving RE as *hard* are those of cognitive nature (i.e., understanding), I have included proportionately more examples of such justifications on the grounds that they can, to a large degree, explain children's poor story recall and lack of understanding about the way in which a recalled story relates to God.

Children's statements

Understanding

- Because I don't know what we have to do (age 5).
- I don't really understand all the things that they are talking about (age 5).
- The suras ... Hard to understand (age 6).
- When we sit down and talk about Him. [Why hard?] Because I don't really know what I am doing ... It's hard to concentrate (age 6).
- Because there isn't one thing that you have to know about Allah; there is more than a thousand things. Even when I am 9, I am still going to be learning about God (age 6).
- Because it takes a lot of time to learn about God. [How long?] A couple of years to learn (age 7).
- It's hard to think what to write about Him. I don't know much about Jesus and God (age 6).
- When somebody is reading the Bible to you and you don't know what the words mean (age 6).
- It was hard reading the Bible about Him ... I couldn't understand (age 6).
- It's too hard to understand. [Example?] Like when Jesus told his disciples to drink his blood and bread (age 6).
- Very hard. [Why?] Everything about God no one knows ... Except the angels and the people who have died and Mary. Only they know what God looks like (age 6).
- Well, sometimes when we don't know what we are talking about, if somebody asked you a very extremely difficult question, I would say it would be difficult (age 6).
- It's about the Bible ... there are lots of tricky words and I can't understand them (age 7).
- I think it's difficult ... Because it's hard to take the point of what my teachers are trying to actually say (age 7).
- Like when He was a ghost ... I don't know why it is so hard to think about Him (age 7).
- Understanding the Gospel (age 7).
- I don't understand some of the language (age 7).
- When you try to learn about God, you can't ... you can't speak to Him, because you can't see Him anywhere ... only when you die (age 7).

Memory

- To tell which god lived there ... in the forest (age 4).
- The questions are hard, like which is the first god (age 5).

- Remembering all the stories … all the details (age 6).
- The daily puja, every day. [Why hard?] Because I forget to do it (age 6).
- If somebody writes something about Allah and you have to know it by heart … that's difficult for me (age 6).
- Questions like what god was wearing today and on Monday and things like that (age 6).
- When we learn by heart very long paragraphs in one week (age 7).
- To remember all the stories (age 7).
- To remember things [?] Like in assembly … if they tell me lots of stuff I get confused (age 7).

Drawing, reading and spelling

- The fingers are really hard for me … I am not that good at drawing them (age 5).
- When copying I can't stay on the line (age 5).
- To draw God's face and body … Because I don't know what God's body looks like (age 5).
- Colouring shapes about Allah (age 5).
- When we are writing about gods and we don't know how to spell their names (age 5).
- Koran. [Why hard?] … I can't read (age 5).
- Hard is the hadith … Because they only have it in Arabic but they are in tiny, tiny writing (age 5).
- Difficult is when you don't know how to spell stuff. What is easy is if you have a picture that you can colour in (age 6).
- The hard bits are when we try to read long Hebrew words and the easy bits are when we read short Hebrew words (age 6).
- Some words we don't really understand because we are small and they are big words that we never heard before (age 6).
- Reading the Bible … It has different kinds of words that are quite hard (age 7).
- Reading about God in another language [?] Gujarati and Hindi (age 7).
- Writing Hebrew words and practising your Hebrew prayer (age 7).
- When you read some hard words it's difficult to join them together (age 7).

What is worth noting about the examples above is the ability of children aged 5 to 7 years to specify the obstacles of cognitive nature for not being able to recall a story. Whilst it is common in the educational literature to attribute children's difficulties in making sense of RE content to their inherent conceptual limitations (e.g., Bastide, 1992; Grimmitt, 2000, 2008; Kay, 2002; Wenger, 2001), it is important to consider first whether the teachings given to young children include the necessary explanations for novel terms and unusual events. For instance, many children in the study made it clear that RE stories are often presented in assemblies, where there are no opportunities for them to ask questions (e.g., "We are not allowed to talk in assembly", age 6). Restrictions of this kind prevent the teachers from noticing gaps in children's understanding which, in turn, precludes subsequent retention in children's memory of the stories heard in RE. Thus, when I asked a 6-year old who struggled to recount a Bible story, why the story was difficult to remember, he replied: "God created two people and told them not to eat the delicious fruit but they did and had to leave their home". The child simply couldn't see why eating a piece of fruit could be a cause for eviction from one's home. In other words, the elements of the story that convey its very meaning were not included in the lesson. Other children highlighted similar struggles: "They [stories] are not difficult for me to read, they are difficult to understand" (age 6) and, likewise, "When the story tells you something and then it's hard to get it in because you don't know what it means that much" (age 7). Yet, understanding the meaning of many RE stories, notably parables, is only possible with some educational help, even in the case of adults, because the events in the stories are not a part of one's everyday experience of the world, especially that of young children's.

In addition to children's frustrations because of not understanding the meaning of RE stories, other components of their school RE may also have an impact on children's motivation for learning in this domain. As mentioned earlier, some of the skills expected of young children (e.g., drawing) are not directly relevant to their RE learning yet younger children come to see them as its main component. It would therefore be pertinent to consider what effect children's difficulties in mastering skills such as drawing might have on their overall RE learning experience. Needless to argue, the answers to such questions ought to be empirically founded, that is, research-based. Information obtained directly from children is of essence when considering whether the currently prevailing conception of primary school RE with its emphasis on social and cultural issues can actually respond to young children's cognitive needs in the religious domain as revealed in their own questions about God (Chapter 5).

To summarise thus far, apart from the linguistic challenges specific to the different faiths, young children's reasons for perceiving RE as *hard* include both conceptual (i.e., understanding, memory) and non-conceptual demands (e.g., lack of drawing skills, reading small size of letters). Conceptual difficulties merit particular attention because they are often construed in the wider literature as attributable to children's inherent cognitive-developmental limitations, which are said to prevent them from acquiring and understanding abstract concepts but, instead, bias them towards crude anthropomorphism, i.e., representing God as a kind of human. Although this particular concern may seem most relevant in relation to Christianity and Hinduism, where RE input often includes explicitly anthropomorphic content, young children from all religious backgrounds can occasionally appear to be biased to anthropomorphism.[6] Thus even Jewish and Muslim children in the current study occasionally stated that there was more than one God, justifying such statements by citing God's different names (e.g., Father, King), or implying that God is synonymous with other divine or godly beings. Certain aspects of RE input may indeed contribute to children's uncertainty about the relationship between God, on the one hand, and the figures such as Jesus, Messiah, Moses, Mohammed, Prophet, as well as any of the particular gods, on the other. Yet, we shall see in Chapter 4 that none of this apparent anthropomorphism or polytheism seems to interfere with young children's confidence that there is only one God when it comes to their understanding of the natural world and answering questions about its different characteristics and its origin.

Whilst children most often identified conceptual reasons for experiencing RE as hard, a number of children across the different schools and age groups occasionally mentioned *moral* concerns for describing RE as hard, regardless of whether those concerns emanated from their own experience or from the RE content that they had learned about. The following three examples of children's views serve to illustrate the connection:

- It's hard being good to Allah ... It's hard (age 5).
- It's a bit hard to do but it's quite easy to listen about God. [Example?] I can't quite understand why to love our enemies who try to hurt us and stuff ... Jesus loved his enemies but I just wonder why (age 6).
- When you are naughty is hard. [Example?] Hard to share my play station with my baby brother (age 6).

Young children's readiness to associate religion with morality is worth noting given that the link between moral and religious understanding has not been at the forefront of recent psychological research and thus remains a neglected topic in contemporary developmental psychology.

Finally, children's reasons for perceiving RE as an *easy* subject are of interest, too. While most of those reasons are not directly RE-relevant (e.g., getting house points; meeting friends and siblings from other classrooms in school assembly; receiving awards), in a few instances children did give RE-relevant responses, such as when implying that just knowing what kind of a being God is makes RE an *easy* learning topic for some 5- to 7-years old children.

- That Allah made everyone ... And He made the world (age 5).
- Quite easy. I've actually known God since I was one (age 6).
- To understand what is God (age 7).

One comment to make at this point already (more in the concluding chapter) is that, contrary to the claims frequently aired in the media that children in faith schools are exposed to too much of religious instruction ("brainwashing"), children's statements quoted in this chapter do not corroborate those concerns. For one thing, it seems that young children do *not* receive sufficient explanation or interpretation of the RE material that they are introduced to so as to enable them to reach the point of understanding it, in contrast to their learning experience in most other school subjects. For another, 5- to 7-year olds from the same faith school can have diverse views about the same issues whilst at the same time sharing important similarities with the views held by children from different faith schools. Neither of these patterns could be explained in terms of indoctrination but instead points to developmental similarities and differences of cognitive nature in young children's responses to RE.

If the RE interviews had stopped at this point, that is, after obtaining children's responses about their experience of the different aspects of school RE, one inescapable conclusion would be that the evidence presented in this chapter is consistent with the arguments in the educational literature, namely, that RE is simply beyond the cognitive capacity of 5- to 7-year olds. For data described in this chapter do indeed suggest that children of this age have difficulties understanding and remembering RE content and hence seem to derive little cognitive benefit from school-based RE. Yet such a conclusion would be difficult to uphold in light of what developmental psychology has documented about young children's cognitive development. Given the volume of psychological research on the emergence of abstract concepts in pre-verbal infants, and on pre-schoolers' inferential reasoning in different cognitive domains (e.g., R. Gelman & Baillargeon, 1983; Goswami, 2002; Mandler & Mc Donough, 1993; Spelke, 2000; Wellman & S. Gelman, 1998), it is not immediately obvious why children should have conceptual limitations in this area of their school learning but not in the other subjects that also presuppose an ability to handle abstract concepts. It thus seemed imperative to seek further evidence from the participating children about their potential for understanding abstract concepts of specific relevance to RE and thereby gain a more objective picture of their potential for deriving educational benefits from the subject. I thus ended each interview by asking the children if there were any questions about God that they had and would like to find out about. This step proved to be an exceptionally fruitful and informative way of learning about the 5- to 7-year olds' interest in the topics belonging in RE and which thus may have significant potential benefits in advancing their cognitive development. Those data are described in Chapter 5, where we look at the main sources of young children's concepts of God. In the next chapter, we will consider children's understanding of the physical world as one of the major sources of their early concepts of God.

Notes

1 School denomination in the current book refers to the type of children's school, whether faith or non-faith.
2 Kodesh means holiness, sanctity or divinity. Definition provided by a member of RE staff.
3 Deen means a collective system of life or way of life in Islam. Definition provided by a member of RE staff.
4 Recall was "detailed" when the narrative seemed coherent and/or when I told the child that they did not need to continue beyond a certain point.
5 See Petrovich (2019) for a brief review of the current approaches to the study of prayer in young children.
6 Not only children but eminent philosophers, too (see Petrovich, 2019, for a review of research on anthropomorphism).

Chapter 4

Everyday religious understanding: The natural-theological reasoning test

Two components of children's everyday or untutored religious understanding are of interest in this book: ontological knowledge[1] and cosmological reasoning. The former pertains to one's knowledge about the world and its most basic categories of existence (e.g., animals, plants, artefacts) while the latter involves one's reasoning about how the world and matter itself began. According to philosophers, the most basic categories of ontological knowledge are in the form of dichotomies (Emmet, 1966); for instance, animate-inanimate, mental-physical, natural-artificial and the like. I will first address children's understanding of the natural-artificial dichotomy, followed by their understanding of the animate-inanimate ontological distinction. Although the two dichotomies often overlap, the main difference between them consists in the criterion used to categorise objects or entities within each. Thus the natural-artificial dichotomy is based on a single causal criterion, which is also extrinsic to an object's boundaries and accounts for its primary or ultimate origin. In contrast, the criteria that define the animate-inanimate dichotomy are intrinsic to the objects (i.e., are species-specific) and include causal mechanisms inherent in the objects' natures, thus explaining their antecedent-derived origins. By virtue of being defined in terms of a single causal criterion, the natural-artificial dichotomy is more comprehensive and inclusive than the animate-inanimate one. I therefore suggested (Petrovich, 2019) that the natural-artificial dichotomy represents a rudimentary theory of the world and a key component of natural-theological understanding in both children and adults. Put differently, its two mutually exclusive ontological categories – natural and artificial – imply that the dichotomy is a fundamentally correct and coherent understanding of the physical world. Importantly, only a correct understanding of the world (i.e., its structure and origin) can give rise to credible cosmological and theological conjectures at any age.

Children's ontological knowledge

In the current study, children's ontological knowledge was assessed in two tasks – Origin and Animacy – by means of a picture test (henceforth

DOI: 10.4324/9781003004639-4

"natural-theological reasoning test") that consists of realistic images (i.e., photographs) of different natural and artificial objects (12 in total), representative of the variety existing in the world (i.e., animals, plants, inanimate natural objects and artefacts). Some objects in the set were familiar to children and some were unfamiliar (i.e., children did not know what they were). Previous studies with children of the same age in Britain and Japan confirmed that prior familiarity with an object did not affect children's ability to identify it correctly as natural or artificial (Petrovich, 2019) so that object familiarity was not included in further analysis. In the current study, children from all the different schools and age groups were indeed able to make a plausible guess about an item's identity as either natural or artificial even when not knowing what it is, thus replicating the earlier findings. The laminated photographs of objects were presented in different combinations of two items (i.e., task conditions) and placed in individual envelopes. Following a brief demonstration of an exemplar set of stimuli, children were instructed to take one envelope at a time and answer a number of questions about the objects inside. The questions about the objects pertained to the objects' origins (Origin Task) and their animacy status, i.e., whether an object is alive or not alive (Animacy Task).

The same children who took part in the RE interview (described in Chapter 3), were tested individually in a quiet area of their school. A key feature of the procedure was to tell children that they should answer the questions as they really thought because I was interested in finding out what *they* think even if they have not learnt about the matter at school or talked about it before. Following the two tasks, children were asked to answer two cosmological questions (details below) and, finally, select one of the three representations of God that they agreed with (details in Chapter 5). The point of asking children about God in the same testing session was to ensure that their reasoning about God was situated in the context of their knowledge about the physical world.

Origin Task

The origin questions were both factual (i.e., how the object shown in the picture came into being) and speculative (i.e., how the first ever object of the same kind, not shown in a picture, came to be). The former question deals with antecedent-derived causal mechanisms of origin (*derived*) and the latter with an object's first coming into being, that is, before the existence of any such item (*primary*). Both types of origin were tested by a forced-choice question format, whereby children received three possibilities from which to select one that they agreed with and do so in connection with both natural and artificial items. In the case of natural objects, the choices for *derived origin* of X (e.g., "*this* dog") were "Made by People", "Born/Grown" and "In Some Other Way", while for *primary origin* (i.e., about "the *first ever* dog") the options were "Always

Existed", "Made by God" and "In Some Other Way". In the case of artefacts, the options for both concepts of origin were "By people", "By God" and "In Some Other Way". It is important to point out that one of the options was always correct, one incorrect, whereas the third was open-ended, allowing children to respond in their own words. The order in which children were asked about the natural and artificial items varied across children but all were asked about antecedent-derived origin first. Following a response about an item's origin, children were asked to provide justifications (i.e., reasons) for their particular choices. Justification responses are of interest because they can provide additional information about children's causal knowledge and understanding and as such verify the coherence, or lack thereof, in children's knowledge about different kinds of existence in the physical world.

The natural-theological reasoning test thus yields quantifiable and directly comparable data from children of different religious and cultural backgrounds regarding their (a) knowledge about the physical world as consisting of different categories of object (natural, artificial, animate and inanimate) which are characterised by different causal mechanisms; (b) ability to reflect on the world in a manner that is characteristic of most religious traditions (i.e., consider different causal origins of existing objects and answer questions about the beginning of the world and primary matter; and (c) capacity to form concepts of God in the context of processing everyday information about the world. In short, the aim of the test in the current study was two-fold: First, to determine whether knowledge of the physical world provides a context for inferring God as a causal agent among children from different types of school – faith and non-faith. If so, the data would replicate the previously obtained findings with children aged 4, 5 and 6 years from Britain and Japan regarding the same aspects of causal reasoning. Its second aim was to identify any consistencies and/or discrepancies between children's concepts of God in the context of their everyday reasoning about the physical world, on the one hand, and in the context of RE as revealed in their experiences of school RE, on the other. A more detailed description of the test, together with a set of illustrations, can be found in Petrovich (2019).

In total, 398 children aged 5, 6 and 7 years from 12 faith schools and one non-faith school were tested in the four conditions of the Origin Task: Natural Derived, Natural Primary, Artificial Derived and Artificial Primary. Statistical analysis of children's responses (ANOVA) according to age, sex, and school denomination revealed that boys and girls did not differ in their performance nor did children's sex interact with any of the other variables. All the remaining analyses reported in the chapter focused on children's age and school denomination as the main between-subject factors.

As expected, children aged 5, 6 and 7 years discriminated reliably between natural and artificial objects according to the objects' origins. Children's grasp of *natural* and *artificial* as two dichotomous groupings is significantly higher than would be the case if they were responding randomly or based on

Table 4.1 Mean numbers of correct responses (out of six) and standard deviations (in parentheses) in the four conditions of the Origin Task according to age

Age	*Natural Derived*	*Natural Primary*	*Artificial Derived*	*Artificial Primary*
5	5.12 (1.21)	4.40 (1.58)	5.38 (1.36)	3.56 (2.23)
6	5.31 (0.93)	4.80 (1.38)	5.75 (0.58)	4.64 (1.88)
7	5.52 (0.81)	5.02 (1.14)	5.83 (0.57)	5.08 (1.62)
Total	5.31 (1.01)	4.73 (1.41)	5.65 (0.95)	4.40 (2.04)

chance (i.e., scored 3 or less) and in a few instances (notably Artificial Derived) it approximates the ceiling or score 6 (Table 4.1).

The effect of origin was highly significant (p = .000) in that children consistently scored higher on derived (M = 5.48, SD = 0.98) than on primary origin (M = 4.57, SD = 1.73). There were also significant interactions between the concept of origin and children's age (p = .000) as well as between origin and school denomination (p = .004). Whilst the effect of object was not significant as such, it did influence children's performance in combination with origin (p = .000) and children's age (p = .027). These multiple interactions indicate that, although all children performed better on artefacts than on natural objects, this pattern was not uniform but varied according to both age and origin condition. As Figure 4.1 shows, the difference is the greatest between children aged 5 and the other two age groups, and especially in Artificial Primary condition.

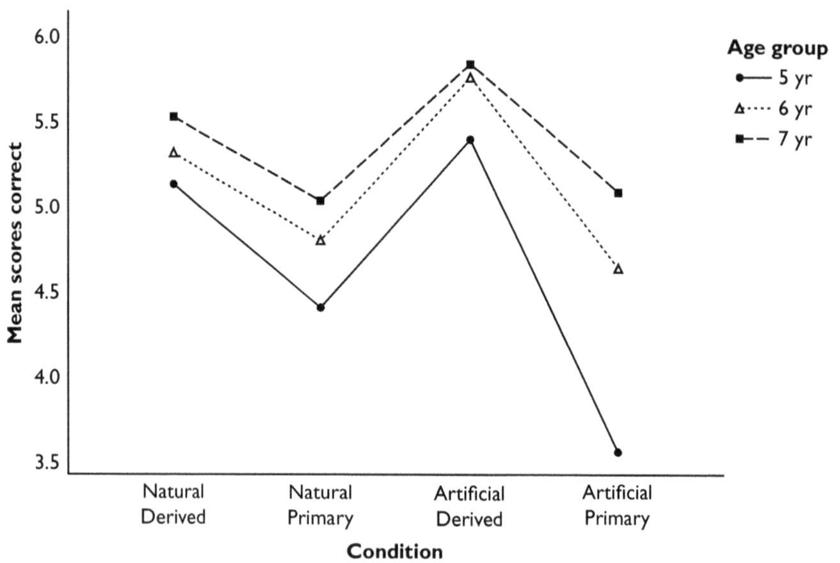

Figure 4.1 Mean numbers of correct responses (out of six) in the four conditions of the Origin Task according to children's age.

Analysis of data according to children's schools revealed a similar pattern of results to that observed according to children's age (Figure 4.2) and helps explain the interaction between origin and school denomination ($p = .004$), which occurred because 5-year-old Hindu and Muslim children scored less than the other 5-year olds in one of the four conditions (Artificial Primary). This is not surprising given that many children from those two backgrounds speak English as their second language. Children's developing language may also account for Muslim children's higher scores on Natural Primary than on Natural Derived, contrary to the overall trend, because identifying a natural item's primary origin (i.e., "made by God") is linguistically simpler than stating the same item's intrinsic or antecedent-derived mechanism of origin. It is of interest to point out that the overall trends found in children's performance in the current Origin Task are very similar to those observed with British and Japanese children of the same age as shown below (Figures 4.3.1 and 4.4.1 in Petrovich, 2019). Such similarities imply that British children from religious schools do not differ in their understanding of diverse objects' origins from British children who attend non-religious schools and nor do they differ from Japanese children who do not receive school-based RE and who live in a culture that does not commonly deal with questions about natural objects' primary origins. Cross-cultural similarities of this kind suggest that children's responses in a given task imply universal reasoning patterns or tendencies.

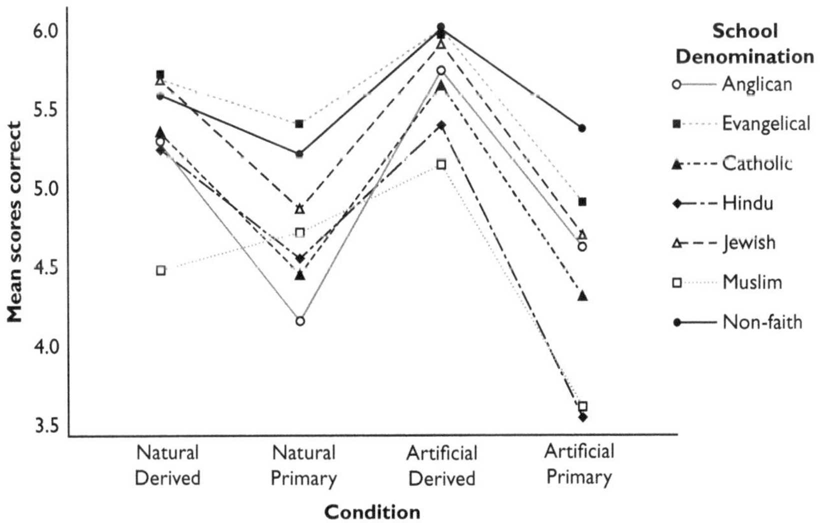

Figure 4.2 Mean numbers of correct responses (out of six) in the four conditions of the Origin Task according to children's schools.

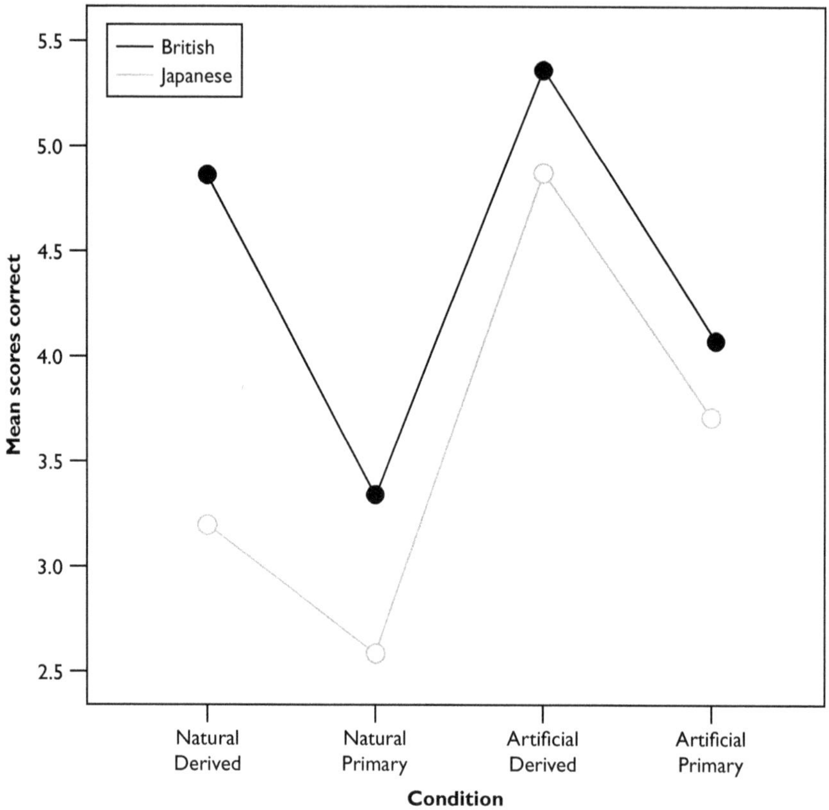

Figure 4.3.1 Reproduced with permission from Petrovich (2019).

Whilst children's better performance on artefacts than on natural items is consistent with the findings reported in many other studies, I suggested a different explanation for this discrepancy than that offered by other authors (e.g., S. Gelman & Kremer, 1991). More specifically, previous studies of children's concepts of natural origins have argued that young children find natural objects' origins harder to explain because they lack knowledge about different objects' intrinsic causal mechanisms (i.e., antecedent-derived origin); conversely, they find it easier to explain the origin of artefacts because children are familiar with its source, i.e., human action. Yet, these two concepts of origin (i.e., intrinsic causal mechanism vs. human action) are fundamentally different ways of explaining origin in that the former are species specific and thus vary according to each natural kind whereas human action is the same and only source of origin of all kinds of artefacts; as such, it accounts for their primary or ultimate origin (artefacts do not have derived origin). Thus, in contrast to artefacts, which have a single origin explanation (human action), natural

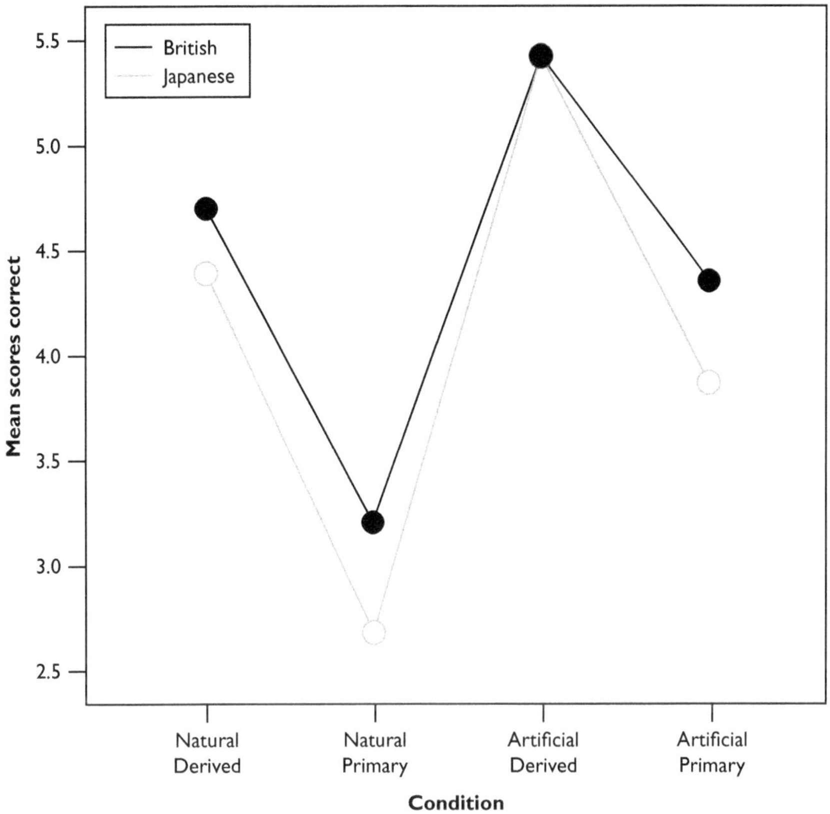

Figure 4.4.1 Reproduced with permission from Petrovich (2019).

objects can be meaningfully explained in both senses of origins: antecedent-derived *and* primary. Crucially, whilst natural objects' derived origins imply diverse or distinct species-specific causal mechanisms, which are *intrinsic* to the objects, the source of primary origin of both natural and artificial objects is always object-*extrinsic*. Thus my point that, in order to identify different natural objects' origins correctly, children need to know which of the two concepts of origin to use as the criterion. Without an explicit understanding of the correct origin criterion, children's strategy appears to vary according to the natural object in question. They are thus more inclined to explain some natural objects' origins in terms of their intrinsic or antecedent-derived causal mechanisms (e.g., "Born from its mother", "Grown from seeds") while other objects, such as inanimate natural, they more readily explain in terms of primary or extrinsic origin (e.g., "Made by God"). What makes artefacts easier for children to explain is the fact that artefacts only have one origin, i.e., human causal activity, so that there is no ambiguity for them to resolve when explaining the origin of such items. In contrast, each natural object presents children with a difficulty of first having to construe the intended meaning of the origin question and then answer it correctly. Indeed, children's lower scores in the Artificial Primary condition additionally corroborate the hypothesis above by showing that artefacts are not always easier to explain by origin but depend on the concept of origin that the question implies. Hence, when asked to explain artefacts' *primary* origin, which implies that such items can have two kinds of origin, children tend to see it as a trick question. Another reason for children's lower score in Artificial Primary condition is in the manner of how some of their responses were scored as incorrect. For instance, there is a notable trend among young children to attribute the first artefacts to God rather than "the first people" on the grounds that the first people didn't know how to make them or didn't have the materials (e.g., metal, paper). While factually incorrect, such responses are not without interest because they resemble Platonist Ideas or Pre-existing Forms.

Animacy Task

Children's understanding of animacy, or the animate-inanimate distinction, has been studied in developmental psychology more extensively than their understanding of the natural-artificial dichotomy (e.g., R. Gelman, 1990, 2002; R. Gelman, Spelke & Meck, 1983; S. Gelman & Opfer, 2002; Golinkoff, Harding, Carlson & Sexton, 1984; Hatano & Inagaki, 1994; Leddon, Waxman & Medin, 2008; Margett & Witherington, 2011; Massey & R. Gelman, 1988; Richards & Siegler, 1986; Simons & Keil, 1995; Springer & Keil, 1989). Researchers have sought to establish when young children acquire this distinction and what factors influence its acquisition. Based on the evidence so far, including my own studies addressing both ontological dichotomies, it is arguable that the animate-inanimate is harder for young children than natural-artificial dichotomy because it can be made on the basis of multiple criteria (e.g., growth, death, movement) rather than just one as is the case with the natural-artificial dichotomy (Petrovich, 2019). Furthermore, many of those criteria (i.e., biological) children cannot discover by themselves but have to learn about from others. It follows that animate-inanimate is less inclusive than natural-artificial dichotomy because it leaves out those objects that do not meet the most common criteria of animacy such as autonomous movement, metabolism and reproduction (i.e., inanimate natural objects and plants). In contrast, *natural* as a category encompasses all natural objects: inanimate, plants and animals, just as the category *artificial* encompasses all and any artefacts. Nevertheless, the two dichotomies frequently and largely overlap as can be seen from children's justifications or reasons for categorising items as animate and/or natural. For example, animals are alive because God made them, or people don't make things that are alive. Notwithstanding such ambiguities, children's understanding of animacy is an important component of their ontological as well as scientific, notably biological, knowledge.

Study of children's understanding of animacy is of additional interest because of the role of language in this domain of children's ontological understanding. Previous findings with British and Japanese participants of the same age as the children in the current study showed that English-speaking children performed better in the Origin Task than in the Animacy Task, whereas Japanese children performed better in Animacy than in the Origin task (Petrovich, 2019). The most likely explanation for this discrepancy between the two nationalities was in terms of the influences deriving from their respective languages. Put differently, multiple metaphorical and other non-literal uses of "live" and "alive" in the English language do not help young learners of English to acquire its basic biological meaning. In contrast, Japanese children aged between 4 and 6 years are in a more advantageous position when it comes to understanding the biological meaning of "alive" because, in the Japanese language, the corresponding term (*ikiteiru*) is used exclusively in the biological sense. It thus seemed appropriate to include a measure of children's understanding of animacy in the current study, not least because the participating children come from different cultural backgrounds and some of them do not speak English as their first or only language.

Children's understanding of animacy was tested by asking them to say if any of the two objects shown in the photographs whose origin they had just identified is "alive" and then provide justifications for their animacy responses on a selected number of items regardless of whether they were correct or incorrect in identifying them as animate or inanimate. Results (Table 4.2) showed that it was easier for all three age groups to identify correctly artefacts ($M = 4.67$, $SD = 2.24$) than natural objects ($M = 4.10$, $SD = 0.96$) according to animacy, $t\,(397) = -.67, p = .000$. Further, a significant age-related progression between 5 and 6 years of age occurred in relation to natural objects ($p = .000$) but not in relation to artefacts ($p = .229$). On the other hand, there is a greater variability (standard deviations) in children's understanding of animacy in connection with artefacts than natural objects, which indicates that children of the same age did not perform at the same level of accuracy.

Table 4.2 Mean numbers of correct responses (out of six) and standard deviations (in parentheses) in the two conditions of the Animacy Task according to age

Age	*Natural Animate*	*Artificial Animate*
5	3.81 (0.96)	4.46 (2.33)
6	4.23 (0.88)	4.64 (2.28)
7	4.28 (0.98)	4.93 (2.07)
Total	4.10 (0.96)	4.67 (2.24)

In contrast to age, children's attendance at different schools did not contribute to significant differences in their understanding of either natural or artificial objects as animate or inanimate (p = .197 and p = .072, respectively). Rather, all children found it easier to identify correctly artefacts as non-living than to differentiate between natural objects as either living or non-living. As Figure 4.3 illustrates, one exception to this general trend are children from Anglican schools whose mean scores in the two conditions are identical (M = 4.09) albeit with different variability within each (Natural Animate, SD = 1.10 and Artificial Animate, SD = 2.54).

Children's greater accuracy when identifying different objects' origin than animacy does indeed suggest their greater dependence on language for acquiring relevant information about animacy than in the case of origin. To verify this hypothesis, children's scores on derived, primary and animacy questions were compared as three separate tasks according to age as well as school denomination. Whilst children's scores in the three tasks differ significantly in terms of children's age (p = .000), there are also significant task by age (p = .003), and task by school (p = .004) interactions. For example, Figure 4.4 shows that all age groups achieved the highest scores in Derived Origin task (M = 5.48, SD = 0.84), and that 6- and 7-year-olds scored higher in Primary Origin (M = 4.56, SD = 1.23) than in Animacy task (M = 4.38, SD = 1.40) whereas 5-year- olds scored higher in Animacy than in Primary Origin task. The same overall pattern is found when children's scores in the three tasks are compared according to their school denominations: Derived Origin is the easiest task for all children, followed by Primary Origin and then Animacy task, with the exception of Hindu and Muslim children for whom Animacy task was slightly easier than Primary Origin task (Figure 4.5).

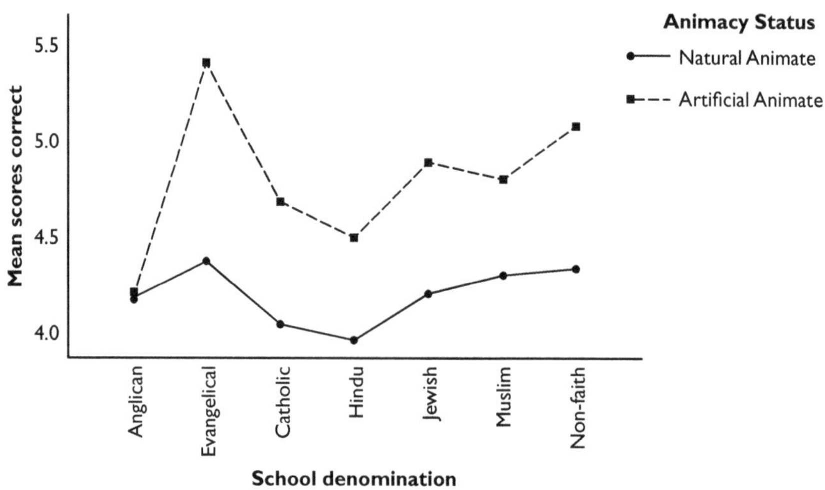

Figure 4.3 Mean numbers of correct responses (out of six) in the Animacy Task according to children's schools.

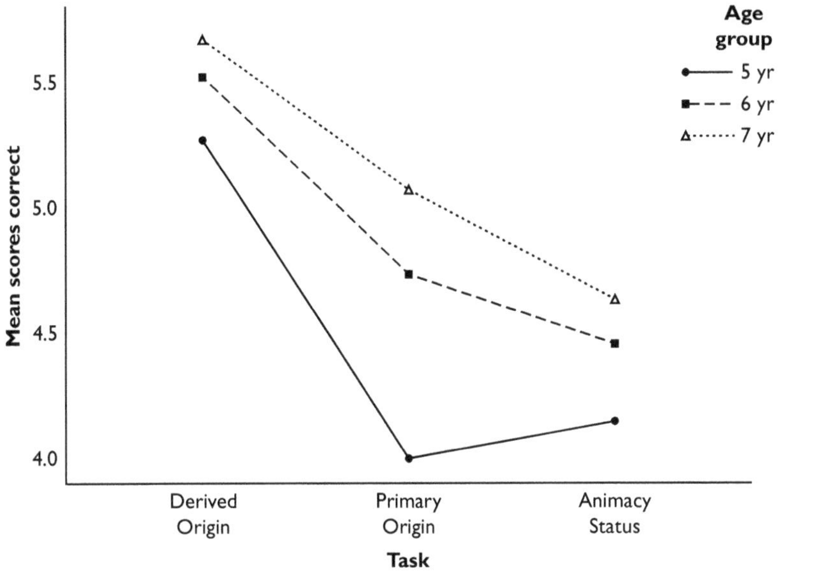

Figure 4.4 Mean numbers of correct responses (out of six) in the Origin and Animacy Tasks according to children's age.

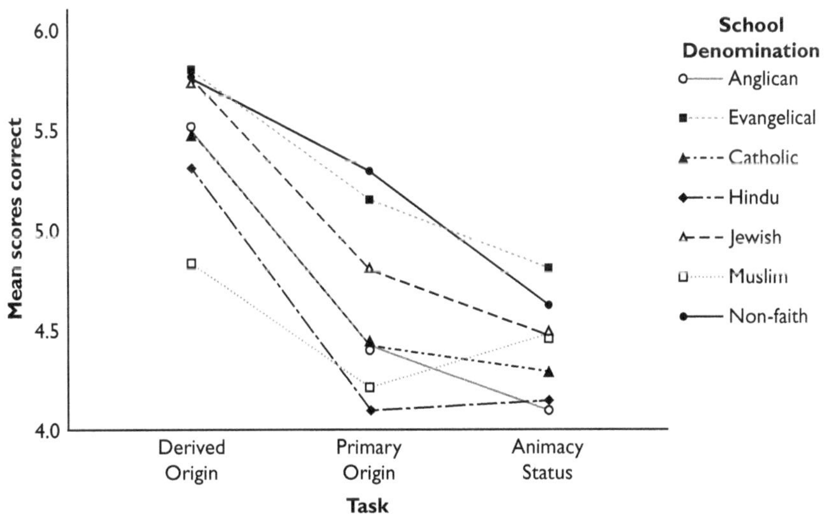

Figure 4.5 Mean numbers of correct responses (out of six) in the Origin and Animacy Tasks according to children's schools.

The results above are also of interest because they point to both similarities and differences found in the earlier studies with British and Japanese children. Namely, while both British and Japanese children performed consistently better on animacy than on primary origin (Figures 4.3.2 and 4.4.2 in Petrovich, 2019), in the current study the majority of children scored higher on primary origin than on animacy. Whilst the influence of language is a highly likely reason for English-speaking children's animacy scores being lower than their primary origin scores, it is also possible that attendance at faith schools confers some advantage when it comes to 6- and 7-year-old children's readiness to respond to the questions about different objects' primary origin. This is not to suggest that children from faith schools are taught to associate primary origin with God; for if they were, their scores in Primary would be higher than in Derived origin condition, which is not the case. Besides, the same children's data described in Chapter 3 did not reveal any such input being received systematically through RE. Last but not least, children from Japan, whose culture has no tradition of associating God with natural objects' origins, also engage in reasoning about primary origin of natural objects. Data in the current chapter are instead consistent with cumulative evidence from psychological research that causal understanding is a fundamental component of human cognition (i.e., a "developmental primitive"; Corrigan & Denton, 1996) and thus plays a key role in many domains of knowledge, including children's understanding of primary origin as distinct from antecedent-derived origin.

In summary, evidence described so far shows that children's understanding of the world as consisting of natural and artificial objects is systematic and theoretical. They arrive at such knowledge by observing the world around them, reflecting on its many aspects and using an abstract causal principle (primary origin) in terms of which it is possible to see any existing object as belonging in one of the two mutually exclusive categories, natural or artificial. The relevance of children's knowledge about the world in which they live to their untutored religious understanding cannot be overstated given the history of science and theology. Without such knowledge being fundamentally correct no credence could be attached to children's speculative reasoning about the world's unobservable properties nor to any inferences that they arrive at in the process of such reasoning. In the remainder of this chapter, we will consider the same children's conjectures in response to the question about how the world itself (i.e., its matter) began as a further source of information about the origin of those ideas.

Children's cosmological reasoning

Although an aspect of causal understanding, children's cosmological reasoning has not been studied in developmental psychology. Cosmological questions pertain to the origin of the world as a whole, i.e., the universe, and its primary matter. In the 1920s, Piaget wrote that even though children aged 2 or 3 years begin to ask about the origins of things, including "Who made the world?" (1977, p. 399), he argued that such questions are "pre-causal" rather than causal, because children do not ask them in the first-cause or "ex nihilo" sense (1925, p. 207) but in accordance with their intuitive belief that a human or human-like being manufactured it. As mentioned earlier, Piaget did not study this form of causal reasoning in children but took for granted the claims about young children's artificialism and pre-causality from Brunschvicg (1949), a French philosopher, and also Sully (1903). There is, in fact, substantial evidence from contemporary developmental research that children of preschool age engage in speculating about the possible and likely causes of a variety of empirical occurrences in an attempt to arrive at complete explanations of what they observe. In the current chapter, we saw that children aged 5 to 7 years from different denominational schools are able to speculate about diverse objects' primary origins, similar to the findings with British and Japanese children aged 4 to 6 years. As well as this, philosophers and scientists alike have often alluded to striking similarities between children and adults in this respect (e.g., Halliwell, 1991; Medawar, 1984). Put simply, when it comes to the question of how matter as such began, children as well as adults, including specialists, have a limited range of possibilities to contend with: (1) "steady state" or an eternally existing universe due to the continuous creation of matter; (2) "the big bang" hypothesis, which states that matter did not always exist but began in an explosion; and (3) existence of an as yet unknown mechanistic cause of the universe (including chance). The third possibility above corresponds with agnosticism or scepticism, which may also embody the view that questions about the beginning of the universe and its matter are not answerable and therefore cannot be rational.

I previously (2019) argued that even young children should be able to understand the differences among the three cosmological hypotheses and articulate their preferences when those are stated in simple language. In addition to the three cosmological hypotheses mentioned above, the test of cosmological reasoning used in the current study also includes a question about God's causal role in the beginning of matter and universe. In short, children received two cosmological questions in this part of the study. The first question asked them to state their preferred view about the origin of matter ("stuff of which the world is made") by selecting one of the three options corresponding with the three main cosmological hypotheses mentioned earlier, namely, (1) eternally existing matter, (2) beginning of matter and (3) uncertainty about whether the question can be answered. As in the earlier study with British and Japanese children, it was important to ensure that children responded in accordance with their own judgments and inferences rather than as part of their school work that might be assessed. I thus told them that even specialists did not always agree about the issues in question so that they should feel free to say what *they* really think. The instruction to children ran as follows:

> Scientists – people who have studied a lot – say that the whole world came from a tiny speck of stuff called "atom", which no one can see and which took millions and millions of years to grow and gradually become different things. But no one is sure how the first speck of stuff came to be. Some people say (a) it had been "always there" (*eternal-matter*), others say (b) it began, probably when God made it (*beginning-of-matter*), and some others say that (c) no one can know for sure and we shouldn't be asking the question (*agnosticism*). What do you think: (a), (b) or (c)? [Repeating each option in an abbreviated form.]

After stating their preferred response option to the first cosmological question, each child then received a follow-up question designed to elicit their views on the role of God, if any, in the origin of matter. The follow-up question asked them to say whether matter or God came first, where the order of mentioning God and matter varied in a random, pre-determined fashion across children. The reason for asking children to say whether God or matter came first was to ensure a correct interpretation of the "always there" option, which many children appeared to use in the sense of "existed for a long time". In all, children provided two pieces of information in this part of the natural-theological reasoning test: First, their preferred cosmological conjecture regarding the origin of primary matter and, secondly, their judgement regarding God's role in the origin of matter.

Origin of matter conjectures

Children's responses to the cosmological questions were analysed by Chi-square tests for independence. The aim of the test was to determine whether children's cosmological judgements were independent of their age and the type of school that they attend. The three age groups did not differ statistically in their responses to the first cosmological question, X^2 (4, N = 395) = 1.18, p = .882. As Figure 4.6 shows, the majority of children in the study, with approximately equal percentages in each age group, selected the beginning-of-matter (Created) response option (total 74%), whilst 14% and 12% of the sample selected "eternally existing matter" (Eternal) and "question not meaningful" or agnostic (Neither) options, respectively.

Children's preference for the Created option is significantly greater than for the other two options. When data were analysed according to children's schools, the overall pattern for the three options is the same as according to age but some differences among the schools within each response category emerged as statistically significant, X^2 (12, N = 395) = 40.41, p = .000, Cramer's V = .000. As Figure 4.7 indicates, the variation among children

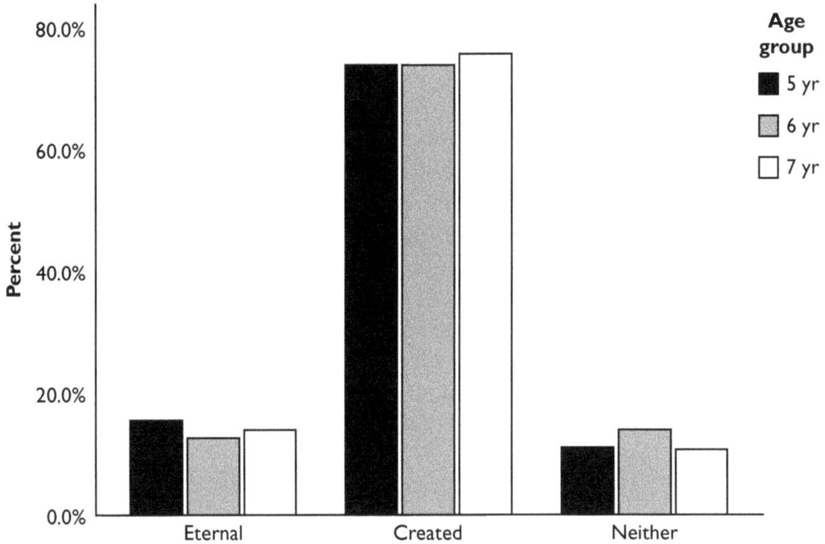

Figure 4.6 Origin of matter: Percentages of children in each age group selecting Eternal, Created and Neither options in response to the first cosmological question.

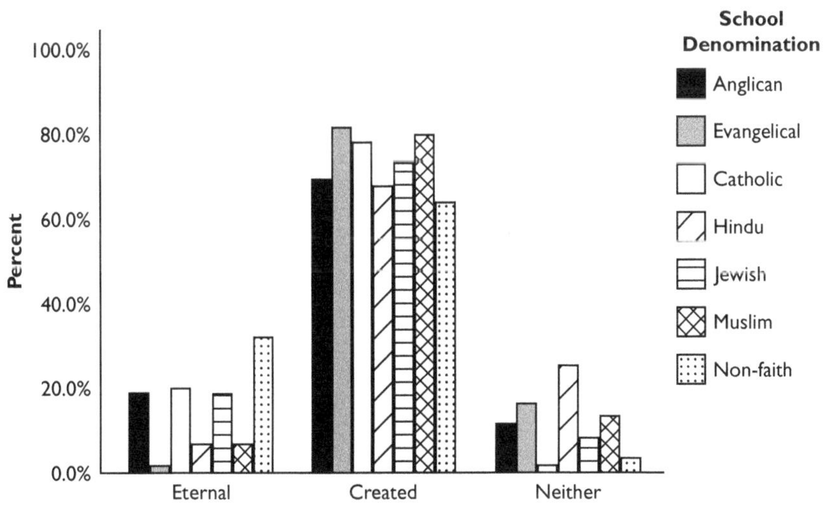

Figure 4.7 Origin of matter: Percentages of children from different schools selecting Eternal, Created and Neither options in response to the first cosmological question.

from different schools is less pronounced in the category Created (i.e., not statistically significant) than in the other two categories; thus, in the category Eternal fewer than 2% of Evangelical pupils selected this option but 32% of the children who attend non-faith school did so.

Similarly, in the category Neither, fewer than 2% of Catholic pupils, but 25% of Hindu pupils, selected this option. The same pattern of responding was found among British and Japanese children who, as mentioned earlier, did not attend faith schools (Petrovich, 2019). What the current children's cosmological judgements show is that attending religious schools does not result in uniform views about matters that involve reflection and speculative reasoning; rather, young children develop ideas about the beginning of matter that may not be consistent with the faith of the school that they attend. Such evidence implies that young children generate ideas and inferences by paying attention to different aspects of the world, which they interpret in accordance with the fundamental causal principles such as determinism, priority and mechanism rather than violating them.

God's role in the origin of matter

In their responses to the follow-up cosmological question, which asks whether matter or God came first, the majority of children in the study (87%) stated that God came before matter (Figure 4.8) but the frequency with which

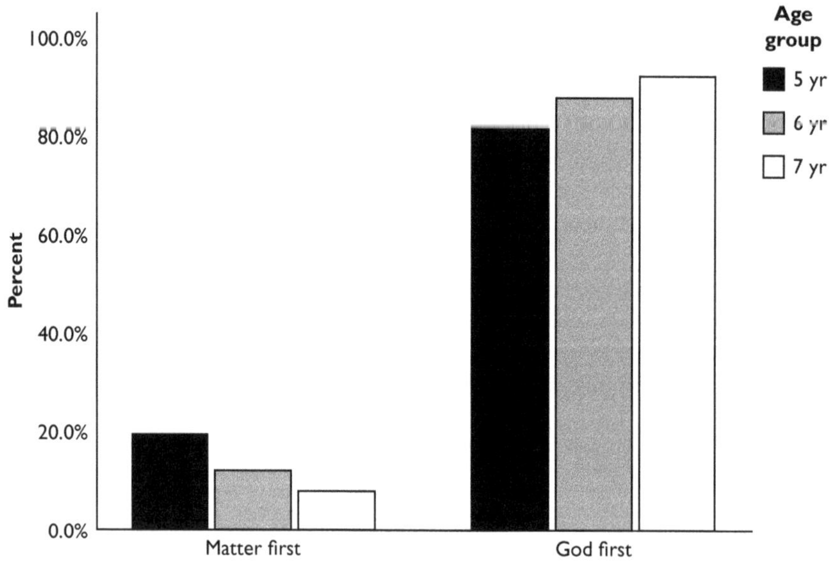

Figure 4.8 God's role in the origin of matter: Percentages of children in each age group selecting "Matter first" and "God first" in response to the follow-up cosmological question.

children aged 5 and 7 years selected this response option was significantly different, X^2 (2, N = 394) = 8.12, p = .017, Cramer's V = .14, that is, 80.9% of 5-year olds, 88.2% of 6-year olds and 92.6% of 7-year olds. Of the 13% children who selected "matter first" option, the highest percentage (19.1%) were children aged 5 years, followed by 11.8% at age 6 and 7.4% at age 7.

Differences according to children's age are consistent with the trends observed in the other parts of the current study, which show that a marked progress occurs between 5 and 7 years of age. When children's responses to the follow-up cosmological question were examined according to their school denominations, the difference between the two categories of response (i.e., God first vs. matter first) was also statistically significant, X^2 (6, N = 394) = 15.77, p = .015, Cramer's V = .20. As evident from Figure 4.9, whilst the overall pattern of children's responses according to the type of school is the same as that according to age, some differences among children's schools emerged as significant.

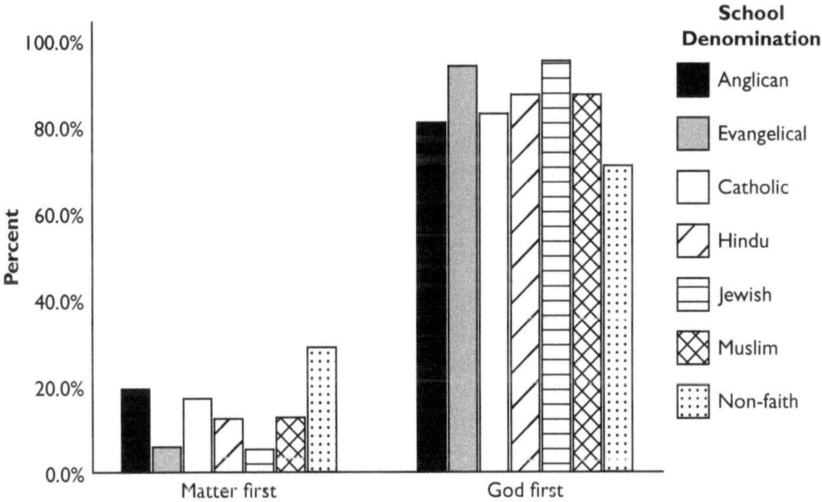

Figure 4.9 God's role in the origin of matter: Percentages of children from different schools selecting "Matter first" and "God first" in response to the follow-up cosmological question.

For instance, children from Jewish and non-faith schools differed significantly in both categories of response (fewer than 5% Jewish & 29% non-faith pupils selected "Matter first"; conversely, 95% Jewish & 71% non-faith pupils selected "God first"). Similar to the findings with British and Japanese participants, a small number of children in the current study suggested alternative views; for instance, that both God and matter ("dust") have always existed; that God made himself out of the dust, God was born from the dust, or that both dust and God were there from the beginning.

Data in the current study appear to be consistent, in part, with an earlier US study with boys aged between 6 and 8 years attending public (i.e., non-religious) and religious schools (Jewish, Catholic, Protestant) and which found that boys from different schools were more similar in causal judgements than the boys within the same denomination (Ezer, 1962). Ezer also reported that children from both faith and non-faith schools offered similar proportions of scientific and "anthropomorphic" answers (i.e., those that mention God), regardless of their denomination and concluded that RE does not impede scientific reasoning.

Overall, children's cosmological judgements described above show important similarities with the data obtained from British and Japanese children as well as adults in that all the participants most often responded to the two cosmological questions in a manner compatible with theism, i.e., that matter did begin and that God had a role in its origin. Similarities between children and adults in cognitive tasks can be interpreted as implying that little or no radical conceptual change occurs in the development of certain aspects of cognition. The form of cosmological reasoning investigated here is a good example of such a developmental pattern, where extensive scientific knowledge is not required in order to make choices between or among the alternative conceptual possibilities. Rather, everyday knowledge and understanding of the world is sufficient to elicit speculative reasoning when seeking to explain its unobservable properties as well as its origin. Current data therefore contradict Piaget's claims, later upheld by some developmental researchers (e.g., Evans, 2001; Kelemen & DiYanni, 2005) that young children have no concept of the "first cause" or ex nihilo origin.

Rather, children's empirical knowledge ("physics") is a starting point for their "metaphysics", i.e., their reasoning about the world's unobservable aspects, not least its origin. Put differently, natural-theological reasoning emerges in conjunction with children's growing knowledge of the world, the latter providing a context for constructing hypotheses and theories about its origin and the nature of its ultimate cause. The three cosmological positions from which 5- to 7-year-old children selected their preferred option correspond with different concepts of God, a topic addressed in the next chapter.

Note

1 In this book, I use the term "ontological" in the sense that this term has acquired in psychology (Keil, 1979), that is, children's concepts of what exists in the world (e.g., animal, artefact, plant) rather than in the philosophical sense, according to which ontology is a branch of metaphysics that differentiates between real and apparent existence. For a more detailed discussion of ontology as a psychological topic, see Petrovich (2019).

Chapter 5

Children's concepts of God: Everyday and RE-based

In the preceding chapter, we saw that young children conceptualise God as a causal agent who is involved in creating entities that human beings cannot do. Causal inferences in general are abstract, where a relationship is established between what is observed (effects) and the typically unobservable causes of those effects. Children's inferences of a causal agent involved in the primary origin of natural objects (i.e., God) are formed in response to the origin questions that arise in their everyday interactions with the physical world. Seeing that inferences of this kind occur across different cultures, including those that do not encourage associating God's causal agency with the natural world (e.g., Japan), it is likely that they represent a universally occurring cognitive tendency (Petrovich, 2019).

In the Introduction to the current book, I said that a key issue of interest in this project is how young children process information about God that they receive through RE and whether this information enhances or hinders their understanding of God's abstractness. I therefore approached the question of children's God-concepts from two angles: (a) representations of God elicited in the natural-theological reasoning test, which are based on children's everyday experience of the physical world (described in Chapter 4); and (b) children's own questions about God, which were elicited during the RE interview (Chapter 3) and are reported in the current chapter. In other words, everyday or natural-theological concept (image)[1] of God is what children acquire spontaneously, that is, independent of any teaching, just as they acquire most other foundational domain concepts, and which constitutes a pre-requisite for processing theologically relevant input that they encounter in school RE. Children's own questions about God, on the other hand, reflect both their wider experience of the world prior to starting formal schooling as well as their understanding of the content transmitted through RE. Put simply, as in most other conceptual domains, both nature and nurture contribute to children's acquisition of the concept of God in any environment. Below I describe in more detail the two approaches used to determine whether young children's concepts of God are theologically

DOI: 10.4324/9781003004639-5

correct, that is, abstract rather than concrete, and describe the main findings of each methodological approach.

Children's everyday concepts of God

Philosophers and early scientists have long argued that human beings infer the existence of God as a causal agent on the basis of their experience of the physical world (e.g., Kant, 1983). Developmental psychology has accumulated a great deal of research evidence which shows that even very young children are able to go beyond the perceptually available information and infer characteristics and properties of objects that are not perceptually evident, such as the objects' intrinsic causal mechanisms and liabilities (e.g., S. Gelman, 2004; S. Gelman & Wellman, 1991; Keil, 2006). More pertinent to the current volume, children's capacity for causal reasoning also allows them to transcend the empirical domain itself and imagine or postulate the existence of absolutely and permanently unobservable entities and causal agents, including God. Following the studies with British and Japanese children and adults (Petrovich, 2019), I used the same procedure in the current research to test children's concepts of God as abstract or concrete (i.e., anthropomorphic). This procedure involves asking each child to state what they imagine or think God to be like, followed by three options from which to choose one that they agree with: "Real man", "Something like a person without a body" or "Something like air or gas". Children were then asked to provide justifications or reasons for their chosen responses by answering the question "Why do you think so?" The aim of the questioning was to see whether 5- to 7-year-olds' responses would reveal an anthropomorphic (concrete) or non-anthropomorphic (abstract) representation of God. Children's responses to each part of the question were scored from zero to 2, where zero indicates a non-informative response (e.g., "I don't know" or other irrelevant); score 1 marks an anthropomorphic or other concrete response whereas 2 signifies an abstract or inferential response. For instance, an abstract concept of God (i.e., score 2) implies that the child had rejected the "Real man" option but selected one of the two other options (i.e., "Something like a person without a body" or "Something like air or gas"). Some children offered abstract responses in their own words, describing God as being akin to light or in other similarly non-anthropomorphic terms. It is important to state at this point that a concrete or literal response (i.e., score 1) does not necessarily imply that children are unable to represent God in abstract (i.e., non-anthropomorphic) terms – even when stating that God is like a man – because their justifications often provide a meaningful explanation for those ostensibly concrete judgements. For example, after stating that their image of God is that of a man, children often justified such a response by citing a specific experience of seeing God on TV, place of worship or pictured in a book. Obtaining children's justifications is thus crucial for a better understanding of the grounds on which they select a concrete (i.e., anthropomorphic) representation of God. Another way of ascertaining whether children's representations of God are abstract or concrete is by considering how consistent they are with the same child's responses in the other parts of the test.[2]

Children's questions about God

In this part of the study my main research questions were, first, how many children in each age and school group do and do not have a question of interest about God. Secondly, how many of their questions imply God's *abstractness* and how many are about *concrete* (e.g., anthropomorphic) features or events associated somehow with God but which do not necessarily imply theological reflection. This distinction, however, is not always simple to verify, such as when concrete features pertain to matters of history or the content of religious texts (e.g., "How the splitting of the sea actually happened, with all the creatures of the sea not dying", age 7). I mention this because it is possible that some of the questions scored as "concrete" underestimate children's theological interests that may actually be abstract but which 5- to 7-year-olds are unable to express verbally as such. Finally, among the children who stated that they did not have a question about God, it seemed pertinent to differentiate between those who say that they are (a) *not interested* in finding out more about God, and those who state that they (b) *already know* (enough/everything) about God. The latter response option prompted a further question, namely, what the child thought was the most important thing about God that they already knew.

In addition to the two approaches above, a third way of determining abstractness of children's God-concepts presented itself in the course of testing children from the Hindu background, the majority of whom referred to "gods" rather than "God" during the RE interview. It therefore seemed proper to ask Hindu children further questions in order to find out how abstract their understanding of God is (see under *One God among many* in this chapter).

Main findings: God image, Image justification and Question about God

Because of some variability in the rate of children's responding on the three measures of abstractness of the God-concept (Image of God, Image Justification, Question about God), I will first provide descriptive statistics (frequencies & percentages) for each of the three measures and then report the results of statistical analysis that allows for comparisons to be made among the three measures in relation to children's age and school denomination.

Image of God

The question was answered by 396 children; this number includes 12 children who said that they did not have any idea what God might be like. Of the 384 children who responded to the question by selecting one of the three representations of God, 210 (54.7%) opted for a non-anthropomorphic representation whilst 174 (45.3%) selected the anthropomorphic option (i.e., that God is like a man) or answered the question in their own words that corresponded with such a representation.

Image justification

Responses were obtained from 367 children; 136 (37.1%) of those were abstract, 165 (45%) were concrete and 66 (18%) were either irrelevant to the question or children were unable to answer the question.

Question about God

In this part of the study, 242 (57.5%) children did have a question of interest about God whereas 179 (42.5%) said that they did not. The latter category is almost equally divided between those who failed to respond (89) and those who stated that they were either *not interested* in finding out more about God or *already knew* enough/everything about God (90). Specifically, 22 (24.4%) said that they were *not interested* whilst 68 (75.6%) stated that they *already knew* enough/everything about God. Among the 242 children who had a question about God, 133 (55%) referred to something concrete albeit associated with God and 109 (45%) were of abstract content.

In order to analyse all three sets of data in terms of an overall abstractness score, only those children's responses that were scored as either abstract or concrete were analysed statistically whilst failure to respond or irrelevant responses were excluded from this analysis. Because the SPSS statistical programme for analysis of variance (ANOVA) takes the lowest frequency available in a data set as the common denominator for the whole set, the comparisons across the variables were performed on data obtained from 177 children, all of whom responded to all three test questions in a manner that could be scored as abstract or concrete.

Children's mean scores on the three tests according to children's age (Table 5.1) and according to their school denomination (Table 5.2) were analysed by ANOVA for repeated measures. No significant differences were found among the three age groups on any one of the three measures of abstractness of the God-concept: Image of God (M = 1.53, SD = 0.51), Image justification (M = 1.49, SD = 0.49), and Question about God (M = 1.44, SD = 0.50).

As Figure 5.1 shows, abstractness of children's concepts of God, and of their image justifications, peaks at age 6 and then reverts to being more

Table 5.1 Mean scores (out of two) with standard deviations (in parentheses) on abstractness of Image of God, Image justification and Question about God responses according to age

Age	*Image of God*	*Image Justification*	*Question about God*	N
5	1.46 (0.51)	1.39 (0.49)	1.41 (0.50)	41
6	1.65 (0.48)	1.60 (0.49)	1.45 (0.50)	62
7	1.47 (0.50)	1.46 (0.50)	1.43 (0.50)	74
Total	1.53 (0.51)	1.49 (0.49)	1.44 (0.50)	177

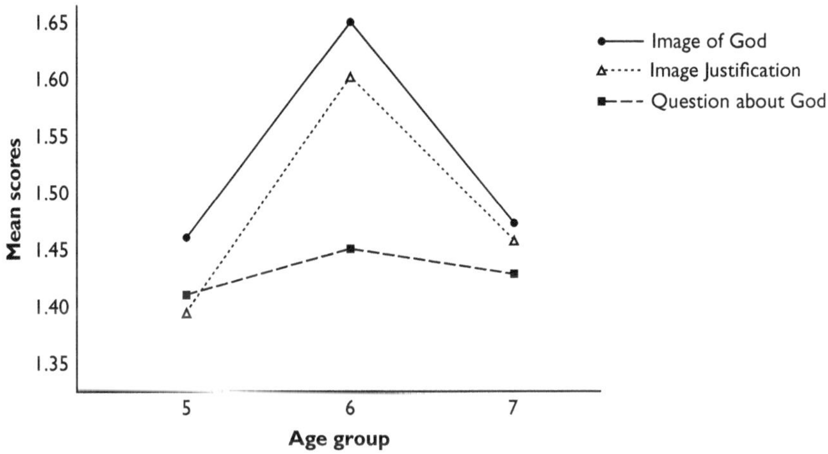

Figure 5.1 Mean scores (out of two) on abstractness of children's Image of God, Image justification and Question about God responses according to age.

concrete by age 7. In contrast, their questions about God show a more even upward trend with age. Analysis of the same data according to children's schools revealed a significant overall effect of type of school (p = .007) and one-way ANOVA confirmed that the effect of school was significant on both children's concept (image) of God (p = .000) and on their questions about God (p = .013) but not on their justifications.

Table 5.2 indicates that the biggest difference in children's mean scores on the Image of God is found between children from Jewish (M = 1.80, SD = 0.41) and those from Hindu (M = 1.31, SD = 0.47) and non-faith schools (M = 1.31, SD = 0.48). Children's mean scores for abstractness of their questions about God are most different between Anglican (M = 1.67, SD = 0.48) and non-faith (M = 1.25, SD = 0.45) school children (see also Figure 5.2).

Overall, the findings described above are consistent with my earlier suggestion that children's concepts of God, whether on the Image of God test or

Table 5.2 Mean scores (out of two) with standard deviations (in parentheses) on abstractness of Image of God, Image justification and Question about God according to school denomination

School	*Image of God*	*Image Justification*	*Question about God*	*N*
Anglican	1.67 (0.48)	1.59 (0.50)	1.67 (0.48)	27
Evangelical	1.62 (0.50)	1.50 (0.51)	1.62 (0.50)	26
Catholic	1.42 (0.50)	1.38 (0.50)	1.35 (0.48)	26
Hindu	1.31 (0.47)	1.41 (0.50)	1.31 (0.47)	39
Jewish	1.80 (0.41)	1.64 (0.49)	1.48 (0.51)	25
Muslim	1.67 (0.49)	1.44 (0.51)	1.33 (0.48)	18
Non-faith	1.31 (0.48)	1.50 (0.52)	1.25 (0.45)	16
Total	1.53 (0.48)	1.49 (0.50)	1.44 (0.50)	177

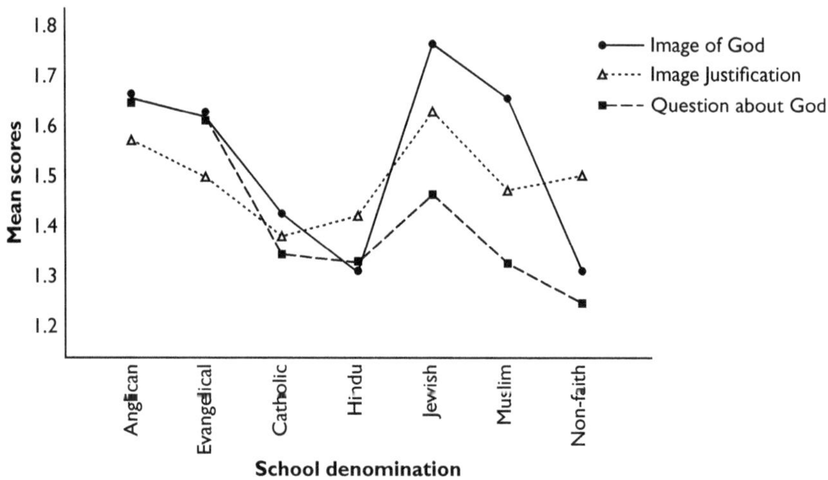

Figure 5.2 Mean scores (out of two) on abstractness of children's Image of God, Image justification and Question about God responses according to school denomination.

in their own questions about God are influenced both by their inferences arising from everyday experience of the world and by children's developing language and impact of formal schooling. Thus, children's rapid vocabulary growth upon starting school seems to explain the difference observed between 5 and 6 years of age whilst their acquisition of new information about God through school RE may account for children's more concrete references to God at age 7 than at age 6.

In other words, after one year at school, children's language development advances sufficiently to enable them to communicate more effectively their understanding of God's abstractness; at the same time, however, they are increasingly exposed to RE content that conveys to them God's characteristics that also apply to human beings. Thus, for example, children frequently mention seeing God in the form of man or being told that God was born, died, wore clothes of a certain kind, interacted with people in space and time, etc. In spite of such manifestly anthropomorphic input, it is important to note that nearly all children's mean scores on all three abstractness measures exceed the values that would be expected if their responses had been random or based on chance (i.e., 50% or score 1). Instead, children's ability to convey their abstract concepts of God is evidenced by their numerous attempts to convey their understanding of the differences between God and human beings. Here I provide a few examples of children's attempts to overcome their existing linguistic limitations. A common strategy for many of them is to make clear that God – even when described in terms that also apply to humans – is different from humans by stating, for example, that God's body is "not like the one in the Mandir" but "invisible" (age 7). Another 7-year old similarly stated that God is "like us but different". When I asked him about the difference, he replied: "He's got ... He's just got a different body from ours ... I think that God has two hearts". A further example of young children's ability to communicate their non-anthropomorphic concepts of God in spite of some significant linguistic constraints is a 6-year-old girl who tried hard and repeatedly to show me with her hands what Allah is like. The exchange went as follows:

> *Allah is like this ... like that, but is over that ... He is like this* [while motioning her hands].
>
> Is that like a person or not like a person? *Not like a person, Allah.*
>
> Where did you see that? *I never see that.*
>
> So, what do you think that Allah is like? *I'll show you* [makes a shape with her hands again and points inside].
>
> Is that like a person or not like a person? *Like a person but different.*
>
> How different? *Just different ... He is like a diamond, you know.*

The examples above testify to young children's ability to communicate their understanding of entities that cannot be referred to in the usual descriptive ways. They also imply that it should be possible to ascertain the presence of an abstract concept of God in young children through systematic questioning about their understanding of the similarities and differences between God and humans. Developmental psychologists have used similar questioning techniques in other tasks which likewise investigate children's understanding of invisible entities such as mental states (e.g., Estes, Wellman & Woolley, 1989). Put simply, the empirical challenge is to devise methods capable of eliciting responses in young children that permit interpretations which are unambiguous and hence conducive to replication through further research.

The finding that children's own questions about God show a more even distribution across the three age groups (i.e., they scored similarly on abstractness of their questions about God) is interesting and it is reflected in the variety of questions about God that 5- to 7-year-olds revealed to be of interest to them. As we shall see from the children's verbatim statements below, there is no type of question that could be found more frequently among any of the three age groups. For instance, the highest occurrence at each age pertains to questions about God's likeness – even after affirming that God is invisible or is like air, gas or some other amorphous substance referred to. Such a similarity across age suggests that children's questions about God are not determined by their formal education but reflect children's wider experience and reasoning about it. Before we consider the examples of children's own questions about God, it is important to account for the responses of the 90 children who stated that they did not have any questions of interest about God, i.e., did not want to find out more about God. Those children were asked about the reasons (justifications) for not having questions about God and the justification question was stated in a forced choice format with two possibilities from which to choose: (1) *Not interested* and (2) *Already knows* enough/everything about God. Table 5.3 indicates that the majority of children selected Already Knows (75.6%) with similarly distributed frequencies across the age groups.

Finally, the children who stated that they already knew enough/everything about God received a further question, "What is the most important thing about God that you know?" as an additional way of determining how abstract their responses might be. From the selection of children's verbatim responses cited below it can be seen that the majority of those are abstract rather than concrete as well as being largely correct, i.e., adult-like.

Table 5.3 Frequencies and percentages (in parentheses) of children's justifications for not having a question of interest about God

Age	*Not Interested*	*Already Knows*
5	13 (14.4%)	21 (23.3%)
6	6 (6.7%)	27 (30.0%)
7	3 (3.3%))	20 (22.2%)
Total	22 (24.4%)	68 (75.6%)

The most important thing about God to know

- That He is everywhere (age 5).
- He looks after us and He makes the whole world for us (age 5).

- Hashem follows us wherever we go (age 5).
- When you pray in the afternoon and in the morning (age 5).
- That He can see everyone (age 6).
- That God is God (age 7).
- That He has magic powers. [What is magic?] To have powers to make things … A tree, a person … actually, the land (age 7).
- That Brahman could give you more lives (age 7).
- That He can do miracles and we can't (age 7).
- That He makes our food … He made the animals to help our food grow … because ladybirds eat other insects that eat our corn (age 7).

Among the 22 children who said that they were *Not Interested* in learning further or finding out more about God, the majority did not elaborate but occasionally complemented the response by citing what they were interested instead (e.g., making models, learning sums). Some, however, gave reasons that appeared similar to the Already Knows responses.

- I thought I knew all the stories (age 5).
- I have heard all of the prophets and the stories (age 5).
- I know all about God. I read stories about Him, everything. I have books about Him in my house … lots of things. All about God in my house (age 6).
- I've got a video of it (age 6).

Questions about God

Among the most frequently mentioned interests in children's questions about God, in all age and faith groups, are those pertaining to God's likeness (e.g., what God looks like) as well as God's inherent invisibility (e.g., why can't we see God). Such children's queries have often been construed by lay adults and specialists alike as exemplifying children's need for concrete representations. This interpretation, however, sits oddly with the evidence from the same children described elsewhere in the current book (Chapter 4, especially), who consistently affirmed that no one can see God. Besides, seeking God's face is the longing of many adults, too, with some notable examples mentioned in the Bible (e.g., 2 Chronicles 7:14 and 30:9). Comparisons between children and adults are a useful way of tracking developmental change, if any, in different cognitive domains (e.g., Coley, 2000; Keil, 1981). The most directly relevant comparisons between children and adults in the current context are those involving participants from Britain and Japan (Petrovich, 2019).

The selection of children's own questions about God shown below could, admittedly, be grouped according to several common themes so that some overlap is inevitable.

God's unknowability: His being and origin

- What I would really like to know about is who God is (age 5).
- I'd like to know why is God called God (age 7).
- I really, really want to know what God is … I mean what He is in His holiness (age 7).
- He is just nothing but He is everywhere … So He is not even air (age 7).
- Who made Him (age 5).
- Where He came from. Do you know where He came from? (age 5).
- I want to know how He made Himself. I don't think it says in the Bible (age 7).
- The first God ever who was born on earth (age 7).
- I want to find out how He looked before He made anything (age 7).
- It's silly, but I don't know how He made himself a God. I always think about it but I can't get an answer (age 7).
- I don't know how Hashem actually appeared. And I am not sure if Hashem had the Torah written already for Moshe to copy it out in heaven before He had created the world. And one more thing: Were the angels created by Hashem or were they just there with Hashem (age 7).
- How did God become a person (age 6).
- I would really like to find out if God is still alive (age 6).
- Was He ever alive (age 7).
- I really want to see what He looks like because I don't know if He is like a light or not (age 6).
- How can you see Him … I want him not invisible but I want Him to stand in front of me so that I can see him … Because He is here, everywhere, but I can't see Him (age 6).
- I want to know how He looks like … and to hear His voice. And I want to see Him how He reads the Koran (age 6).
- I want to find out how He can watch people when they are invisible … In the sky (age 6).

God's causal powers

- I'd like to know how He makes things, like when He made the animals and the earth (age 5).
- How does God make us (age 5).
- How He created the world (age 5).
- How God created the earth … I know about how the animals came (age 6).
- How He got kind of magic … 'Cause He is magic, but I don't know how He got magic (age 5).
- How He does His miracles; that's what I am trying to find out (age 6).
- Why God didn't create anything when the dinosaurs ruled the world.

I'm not sure, but I think it's 'cause He didn't want any people to be eaten by the dinosaurs (age 6).

- I want to know how God made us … the nails, our hearts and everything (age 6).
- I'd like to learn how He made the world. Stuff like that is interesting [not Bible stories] (age 7).
- I'd like to know where He got His powers from (age 7).
- I would really like to know how God made the world entirely. I know that there is a connection between God and science but the scientists … I don't think they understand that. God must have created the stars that created the Big Bang (age 7).
- How God exactly made the world. Some people say there was a place where the first people lived, Adam and Eve in English, but other people, like the scientists, think that it started with a little ball and then the ball exploded … (age 7).
- How God shaked the floor in the tsunami … I really want to know how He makes the sun come, morning and night, how He does it … And I wonder how the moon and the stars are bigger than the world … and space (age 7).
- How He made the chimps evolve into us. That's the only thing I want to learn (age 7).

Death and afterlife

- How … how you become a god. And what happens to you after you die … I know that you go to the sky but I don't know what you become in the sky (age 5).
- When people die, I don't know where they go (age 5).
- When is the day of judgement (age 6).
- What does heaven look like (age 7).
- When people die and are buried, what happens after that (age 7).

God's moral agency

- How does God help you do things (age 6).
- How He helps us … and how He makes it happen (age 6).
- I want to know if God is really a kind person … because He didn't help Joseph in the Bible (age 6).
- How good He is and if He could defeat all the bad guys (age 6).
- If He loves everyone … because there might be someone He doesn't love. [Example?] The devil. [Should God love the devil?] He doesn't have to, but I think He should. [Why do you think so?] Because He is God and He shows His love (age 7).

Communication with God

- If He can talk to us in these days (age 6).
- When we do duah [prayer], does God give it to us (age 6).
- If He knew that when I prayed and closed my eyes that I prayed in my heart and I meant it … That's all (age 7).

Other philosophical-theological questions

- Why was He born for us (age 5).
- How do they know that they are a god (age 6).
- If we could ever see our soul (age 7).
- How was Satan an angel and then turned into bad (age 7).
- How do the gods know what our past is and what our future is (age 7).

Perhaps the most significant finding in this part of the study is the broad range of children's questions about God that they would like answered. Whilst some of the questions clearly arise from the specific educational input that children receive (e.g., How did Moshe speak with God; Why did they kill Him; How did God send the Koran), many of their questions about God arise in a wider context than that of formal RE and are similar to those reported by other authors (e.g., Madge, 1965). Indeed, the very same questions have preoccupied philosophers throughout the history (e.g., Cassidy, 2012). The sheer variety of children's musings about God reveals a great deal about their metaphysical proclivities that no extant RE theory or instruction manual for primary school RE has envisaged. As for children's "childish" questions, they ought to be accounted for by considering the input that children receive, not only from their formal school RE but, also, from their particular cultural environments, the media and the wider society in which they live. Taking children's "childish" questions as typical of early development misrepresents the reality that developmental psychology seeks to explain, namely, children's cognitive capacity within a knowledge domain, in this case theological, by taking account of the conditions under which it emerges and the extent to which it can be influenced by those conditions.

What the evidence described so far shows is that not only were even the youngest children in the study able to convey what they imagine God to be like and reveal their own questions about God, but they were also able to articulate the reasons for holding them. As already pointed out, the significance of young children's questions about God is in their range, which encompasses core metaphysical issues, such as God's ontological nature, divine causal powers, life and death matters, good and evil, cosmology, and the like. Indeed, a whole book could be written based on those revelations in order to give justice to the diversity, originality and coherence of children's theological reflections. It is of developmental-psychological interest that children's questions about God are remarkably similar across age and across different faith schools. That children's statements of this kind are not mere parroting of what they hear from others is evidenced by both the variety of responses within the same religious tradition, and even within the same school, as well as by children's expressions of doubt about some of the content of their RE teaching. For example, a 6-year old said, "I don't really believe in God because who made that God and who made *that* God … and how the first God was made. How was he born? [Have you asked?] My mother, but she doesn't know", while another wondered "If there is really such a thing as God … I don't know if there is but I believe there is Jesus" (age 7).

In light of the evidence described in this chapter, the task for developmental researchers is to provide an account of the conditions present in children's early environments that are likely to give rise to their initial questions about God. Numerous studies by developmental psychologists have documented that even infants and pre-verbal children actively process information about the world in which they live and engage in causal reasoning in the first year of life (e.g., Baillargeon, 2008; Spelke, 2000) while between 3 and 6 years of age they construct theories "through causal reasoning" and engage in theory evaluation (Kóksal-Tuncer & Sodian, 2018, p. 144).

One God among many

I mentioned earlier that an additional source of insight into young children's understanding of the concept of God emerged during the testing, especially of the children from the Hindu background, who commonly referred to "gods" rather than "God" during the RE interview. This presented an opportunity to investigate further how children from this particular background, known for its rich pantheon, conceptualised God's abstractness. I therefore asked each child from this school group "How many gods are there?" followed by the question "How many gods are there in England?" In most cases, I also asked, "Why, do you think, there are so many gods?" A total of 54 children of Hindu heritage answered the first two questions, with the majority of them mentioning a number of Indian gods by name and stating that their total number ranged from 10 or 12 to "zillion". Several children, however, stated that there was one God only and offered explanations why others thought that there were more gods. Children's responses to the question about the number of gods in England were more varied and ranged from one or two (God and Jesus) to affirming that English people had the same number of gods as the Indian people or that one of the two nations had more gods than the other. When I asked them what they thought were the reasons for a different number of gods in England and in India, they most often attributed the difference to the population size in the two countries (sometimes mistakenly stating that more people lived in England than in India), while also suggesting that different gods perform different roles.

In addition to Hindu children, 24 children from the other schools (Anglican, Jewish & Muslim) also mentioned "gods" and in those instances I asked them the same questions that I put to the Hindu children. Their answers were surprisingly similar to those given by their Hindu peers when giving reasons for there being more than one God (e.g., God has different names, can appear in different places, can be known or experienced simultaneously by multiple persons, and the like). Such children's explanations do not constitute evidence for crude anthropomorphism for two main reasons: First, none of the children in the study referred to "gods" when answering the questions about the origins of natural objects and the world as such but consistently referred to "God" in that context. Such a pattern implies that 5- to 7-year-old children appear to conceive of God as the beginning of a causal chain of whatever they are trying to explain. Further, children's justifications for referring to "gods" seemed to suggest that multiple gods represent diverse manifestations of one God, or extensions of the concept of divinity (holiness) to include phenomena that are closely associated with God (e.g., angels, prophets, saints). These are the very issues that merit further and more systematic research than was possible in the current study. Below are some of the examples that illustrate the points just made about what seemed to be a common trend among Hindu children's representations of God when responding to the questions: How many gods are there? and Why do you think so?

- [Lots of gods] Because everyone needs a god (age 5).
- First, there is one God and then … all the gods begin to begin (age 5).
- They [Christians] have a special God in Jesus. It is their forever God (age 5).
- English people have lots of gods, same as Indian people (age 5).
- The same gods are in all the countries … All of the gods are here but some of them are Jesus and some are Indian gods … (age 6).
- Jesus is the real God's son. He was born at Easter but when Easter finishes, he is gone (age 6).
- [A hundred] Because all the time that people go somewhere, God is around you and in your heart (age 6).
- There can't be just one God because there are so many of us (age 6).
- There is one God but he can become other gods and sometimes he takes the other gods out of him and lets them spread in the sky (age 7).
- Just one, with lots of different names. [Why so?] Because people sometimes get bored of one god … they go to another but they still pray to the same God (age 7).
- Some people say there is one God but he has loads of names. That's what I believe. Some other people in my class say there are loads of different gods and they have different names. And some people say there are loads of gods and one of them has different names. I believe in

the first one. And in the Mandir, they think that there are loads of different gods ... Because there are so many pictures of different looks of Him. But there is only one ... That's what we Hindus believe (age 7).
- There is only one God but from him they all split up (age 7).
- The same number [of gods] as in England ... I think it's infinity (age 7).

Although many of the children from the other schools who referred to "gods" corrected themselves when I asked them to specify the number of gods by asserting that there was one God only, a few seemed to think of God and persons close to God as being of the same nature. For example:

- You can't really see Moshe and Hashem because they are everywhere and you can't see them because they are invisible (age 5).
- [Five gods] I know their first names – Muhammed, Yousef, El Hussein ... They were born but Allah wasn't born (age 6).
- There are loads of different gods ... There is the sun-god, the rain-god, storm-god and the hailstone-god and there is a bad god and then there is a normal god. He made the sun, that's the most important ... So, there are six gods. The normal god doesn't have to do everything. There's got to be different gods (age 7). [Church of England school pupil.]

In Chapter 3, we saw that, although the religious traditions included in the project seem to differ fairly substantially in the ways that God can be represented, important similarities emerged in how children aged between 5 and 7 years from those traditions actually process RE information. While many children from Christian and Hindu schools say that they mentally represent God in some concrete (i.e., visual) form, that is, describe or refer to God in human terms, their justifications for such representations unambiguously testify that children acquire those representations as a result of RE input that they receive both at school and informally and which is of a distinctly anthropomorphic kind. Put differently, given the emphasis on Jesus in Christian RE and the multitude of incarnate gods in the Hindu tradition, about whom children learn in their RE, it is not surprising to observe explicit anthropomorphic patterns of responding among children from those backgrounds. It is more surprising to find that similarly anthropomorphic representations can be found among children whose religious traditions discourage any conceptualisation of God in concrete form (Jewish, Muslim). At their face value, such trends among young children could be seen as evidence of crude anthropomorphism in young children (i.e., belief that God is just another human being) as, indeed, many psychologists and educationists mentioned earlier in the book have argued to be the case. Yet, children's justifications (reasons) for holding those representations often reveal considerable sophistication when conveying such concepts (e.g., deliberate resorting to metaphors, analogies and other imaginative tools), all with the aim of indicating their understanding of there being important differences between God and human beings. Some striking examples of this kind were obtained from children in the current study who said that, unlike people, God has lots of eyes or God only has a head but not a body or only giant eyes but no head.

In short, evidence from children presented in this book contradicts the assumptions pervading much of the primary RE literature that young children cannot conceptualise God in abstract terms because they are biased to believing what adults tell them or rely on what they can actually see. When the scoring system used here is taken into account, which, as mentioned earlier, classifies as "concrete" any factual (e.g., historical) questions about events associated with God, children's achieved scores on abstractness may well be an underestimate. Although some of the current data are similar to those reported by Madge (1965), which she obtained from the parents and teachers of 5- to 7-year-old children asking questions about God,[3] Madge interpreted those data by adhering to Goldman's (1964) criteria and concluded that "Children's conceptions of the deity are in the first place founded on human relations" (1965, p. 100). More recently, other authors have similarly argued that only through contact with adults can children learn about God (e.g., Mountain, 2005; Shtulman et al., 2019). The assumption that children's understanding of God depends on the input that comes from adults is pervasive in the educational as well as psychological literature, even when the findings of those studies run counter to those assumptions. For example, whilst Rymarz and Belmonte (2020) set out to investigate children's ideas about Catholic identity, some of the children's questions reported by their teachers were actually about God rather than Catholic identity (e.g., "how do we really know the Bible is the word of God"; "did Jesus really walk on water?", p. 123). Furthermore, children's questions such as "who made God?", "what does God look like?", "where did God come from?", Rymarz and Belmonte classified as "inferior" although a number of the teachers included in the study commented that such children's questions were similar to the questions that they themselves "still have today in many cases" (p. 125). Put simply, it seems that researchers often perceive children's questions as "childish" because they fail to consider the similarity of children's questions to the questions asked by adults, including major philosophers, such as Aristotle, Descartes, Kant or Plato (in Cassidy, 2012, p. 64).

Notes

1 Some authors differentiate between "God image" and "God concept" (Davis, Moriarty & Mauch, 2013) in terms of the role of affect (i.e., attachment) associated with each. In the current book, both "image" and "concept" refer to a mental representation, an idea or conception (*The Concise Oxford Dictionary*, 9th Edition, 1995).

2 When scoring children's responses that seemed ambiguous in this respect, a response was marked as "concrete" if a child had stated either during the RE interview or in the image of God question that they had seen God (in a book, film, place of worship) or otherwise know that God is a man. Conversely, a response was scored as "abstract" if a child had stated in the same tests that God is invisible, is like air, spirit or that no one can see God (cf. Nye & Carlson, 1984, p. 139).

3 How was God born? Did God die? If God was there before the world was made, what did he walk on? If God came as a spirit, how was he born? Does Jesus live inside or around us? Is Jesus God? Is God Jesus' father? How can he be? Why can't I hear God's voice inside me like Samuel did? Does God have hundreds of eyes so he can see everyone? How can God possibly make room in heaven for everyone for ever and ever? Was it holy before Jesus was born? (Madge, 1965, p. 14).

Chapter 6

Teachers' perceptions of young children's abilities for RE learning

Forty-seven teachers (29 Christian, 14 other faiths and 4 non-faith) from the same 13 schools as the participating children were interviewed about their experiences of teaching RE to 5-, 6- and 7-year-olds. The aim of interviewing the children's teachers was to obtain their perspectives on several aspects of the RE process and address some of the issues that were prominent in children's interviews. The most important of those was children's potential for understanding RE content against the background of abundant literature on RE for primary age which puts strong emphasis on children's conceptual limitations as a reason for avoiding to teach any content that involves abstract concepts, including that of God. As argued in the preceding chapters, this rationale is inconsistent with substantial developmental-psychological evidence that even pre-verbal children form abstract concepts in a variety of cognitive domains (e.g., Goswami, 2002; Wellman & S. Gelman, 1992). Furthermore, data obtained from children in the current research do not indicate that such limitations exist, rather the opposite. In many instances, children's statements reveal a capacity for metacognitive insights into the reasons for their lack of understanding of the RE material presented to them, such as not receiving the necessary explanations for novel terms and concepts contained in that material. In order to account for the apparent disparities between children's abilities identified in this study, on the one hand, and the portrayal of those abilities in the RE literature, on the other, it was imperative to consider each side's views as a key factor determining the outcomes of RE learning among 5- to 7-year-old children. Following the reporting of children's findings in Chapters 3–5 in the current chapter I describe data obtained from the children's teachers as they cast additional light on young children's experience of receiving RE teaching and the impact of that teaching on their concepts of God.

When interviewing the children's teachers I sought their views about the following issues: (1) young children's *cognitive (conceptual) abilities* for the subject, especially their understanding of abstract concepts such as God; (2) *usefulness of the teachers' own training for teaching primary RE*; and

DOI: 10.4324/9781003004639-6

(3) teachers' views regarding the main *purpose of school-based RE* for young children.

As anticipated, much useful information emerged from the teachers' interviews, revealing both the similarities and differences among the teachers from the schools included in the project. One of the notable similarities, to be discussed in more detail later, concerns the teachers' virtually unanimous agreement that their professional teacher training did not equip them with knowledge and skills needed for teaching RE to children of primary school age. As for what transpired to be the main difference among the same group of teachers pertains to their views about the purpose of school RE for young children. Broadly, but not exactly, a contrast emerged between Christian, on the one hand, and non-Christian faith schools, on the other, regarding the amount, if any, of multi-faith component in primary RE. The division is not precise in that it disregards the differences among and within the different Christian schools, to be highlighted later in this chapter.

Teachers' views of young children's conceptual abilities for RE

My questions to the teachers about young children's conceptual abilities for RE focused on the issue whether children aged between 5 and 7 years conceptualise God in abstract terms or, rather, spontaneously and naturally think that God is a human being, i.e., form such a concept prior to receiving RE. The majority of 47 RE teachers were of the view that children of this age lack an abstract concept of God but, instead, think about God in concrete terms, typically as a man in the sky or a kind of magician. Only a handful of the teachers thought that children of this age are capable of conceptualising God in abstract terms but lack the vocabulary needed to express such concepts. In a number of cases teachers' judgements were followed by a caveat that, based on their own interaction with young children, the teachers could not be entirely sure if this was the case and some expressed a hope that the current project might provide the much needed clarification ("I would like more research into this … . No research on children's experience of RE", T 13). Below is a selection of the most common teachers' statements regarding young children's conceptual abilities for RE.

Teachers' statements

T 2: Their idea of God is [that of] a solid person … It's just that they can't reach him. If that's their way of relating to God then I reinforce it, it's not such a bad thing. For example, I refer to God as Jesus's dad, a familiar word that wouldn't give them a fear of God.

T 3: Abstract is difficult. But most of them were able to draw their idea of God … Most children were happy to draw God; only two said they didn't know what to do.

T 4: Their concept of God is what we told them … But I'd be very interested to see what the children's response to that question is … Most of the time they think of a man in the sky.

T 8: It is very hard to know what concepts 4-year olds are coming to school with. Man in the sky is probably very common. They acquire abstract concepts at age of 9 to 10 years.

T 10: They can't grasp the idea of a thing beyond time and space.

T 14: Man in the sky, yes … an elderly man. It's not something that they have vocalised but I detected it.

T18: Abstract concepts are difficult. They need to explore things by feeling and touching; you can't touch a spiritual element. Artefacts are useful.

T 19: Concrete … I wouldn't teach them anything abstract.

T 24: It is difficult for young children to believe what they can't see. God is a man in the sky.

T 26: Parental concept of God … Can't acquire that [God-concept] on their own. They don't make a connection between nature and God. They need a person to talk through the connection.

T 31: Children have a concept that God came down on this Earth in the form of a human being. But they depend on RE teaching for an abstract concept of God. The concept of an invisible God is very hard.

T 34: There is no concept of God for the majority of children when they start school but, if they have it, it's a concept of a man in the sky. They have to be helped to undo the image.

T 35: They know that there is only one God but they must give it a body … something in heaven. Even if they are not from a religious home, they know what God is because there is always something around them to tell them about God. So, the only problem is understanding that God has no body.

T 38: A person in the sky, yes. Difficult not to think of a human … Children don't ask, so it's difficult to know.

T 39: [The teacher has seen children discuss God in the context of natural origins] I doubt that very young children can understand abstractness because we refer to God in human pronouns. It's difficult for children not to think of God as a human, something physical.

T 40: Children aged 4 to 7 are quiet, they don't ask questions. Their parents teach them about God before they come to school. The idea that they can't see or hear God is hard for them.

T 41: God is a man in the sky. They can't think of God as invisible but need something solid in their head.

T 43: Abstract concepts are very difficult, they can't think in the abstract. God is a kind of person.
T 44: Man in the sky, definitely. One of the lessons we did recently was "Draw a picture of what you think God is like", and it was all about the beard, long skirts, sandals ...
T 47: Those who go to church (only two or three) know that God created the world but the others use the word God but I don't think they understand who He is or what He does, just a kind of force or power. Many probably think He is a man in the sky.

What is of interest to note in the examples cited above is that even when the teachers had not heard the children say that God is a man, they seemed convinced that 5- to 7-year-old children could only have a concrete or physical (anthropomorphic) image of God until adults correct it later on through formal or informal RE.

In the case of the teachers from the schools with a multi-faith approach to RE, I asked a further question, namely, whether 5- to 7-year-old children understand that RE involves learning about God. Of the nine teachers who replied, no teacher said that this was the case.

Teachers' statements

T 1: They are learning from God ... in terms of Jesus's life story.
T 2: I think they appreciate Jesus as a really helpful person but they tend to associate his power with magic. And I hope that would change towards miracles.
T 3: The guidelines tell you to teach about the Bible but children were quite confused about who Jesus was, who God was, so I didn't follow the guidelines.
T 6: We don't talk a lot about God specifically but more about how God is thought of in different religions. We also give them time to close their eyes and think about what God might be like but very often RE is focused on rituals and practices ... Because of the children's age.
T 10: Yes and no. They wouldn't necessarily see God and religion as the same thing. They don't understand concepts of God is ... The society doesn't understand either but get God and religion confused. Children do believe in the divine but by the age 9 or 10 some of them pick ideas in the society that spiritual is inferior intellectually.
T 12: I don't know ... I don't know.
T 18: No, I don't think they feel it's about the religious element.
T 19: When we do a religious story we talk about feelings ... They bring in God.

I next asked the teachers to comment on several other aspects of their experience of teaching primary RE which likewise imply children's ability to understand religious concepts in abstract terms, such as, for instance, the relationship between God and the other prominent divine or godly beings in their respective religions (e.g., particular gods, Jesus, Moses and Muhammad). Many teachers from the schools teaching Christian RE said that they were aware of children's confusions when it comes to understanding such a relationship (see the statements below). Teachers of Hindu RE similarly reported young children's difficulty with understanding the need for so many incarnations, i.e., why the various gods came down. By contrast, teachers from Jewish and Muslim schools were confident that children did not confuse God, on the one hand, and Moses or Muhammad, on the other.[1] I therefore asked those teachers who were aware of children's uncertainties to comment on the likely reasons for children's apparent confusions. Two kinds of teachers' response were salient and seemed directly related: first, the question of the relationship between God and other divine or godly beings was not being addressed in primary RE so that they couldn't comment; secondly, that children never ask about such a relationship.

Teachers' statements

T 2: We don't focus on that and children don't ask.

T 3: They find God – Jesus relationship very confusing … And I didn't even mention the Holy Spirit [laughs].

T 4: That hasn't cropped up. They see Jesus as God's son in the human form but I haven't delved into that relationship.

T 5: They don't ask.

T 6: They just accept that Jesus is God's son … I'm not sure how they would answer that or how we would.

T 7: Haven't gone into that. They never ask.

T 8: I'm really not sure about that. That's not a great part of what we look at.

T 10: More able children ask some very good questions about the Trinity. I don't think they see God and Jesus as the same. The meaning of a theological concept of Jesus is difficult to understand whereas they can understand that Jesus is a good man and God's son … but for him to be God as well is hard.

T 12: No, that doesn't come up.

T 13: The Resurrection is quite a puzzle to children … I don't think they think too much about the relationship.

T 14: Difficult, especially at Easter when Jesus died. I, personally, find it hard why Jesus died on the cross.

T 15: I leave it to the children to offer their own ideas that I don't know myself. But they don't query deeply.
T 18: They think of them as any father and son; that gives them a visual picture because children need something concrete.
T 20: They don't ask, it's a Gospel to them.
T 21: That can be difficult for them to grasp. In all my years I've only had one child who understood that God can be three in one.
T 22: Father–son, think of daddies ... God the Father is probably a daddy to them.
T 23: Difficult to teach. I don't mind Jesus and God being interchangeable but I wouldn't want to put them through catechism.
T 24: Jesus is like a human son of his father.
T 25: Physically son of God.
T 26: Jesus is easier, concrete.
T 27: Father and son, nothing deeper.
T 29: Confused about Mary's role – bride of Jesus. Trinity is even harder. Even adults need a supportive father figure.

Whilst the examples quoted above may be seen as evidence of primary RE teachers' insufficient subject knowledge (i.e., religious studies, theology) to allow them to address the question of God – Jesus relationship, the lack of psychological education, especially teachers' lack of familiarity with developmental research that investigates young children's conceptual abilities in different knowledge domains is a far greater problem to which I will return later in the book.

Another way of gaining some insight into the teachers' implicit expectations of their pupils' abilities for RE learning was to ask them to predict what *questions about God*, if any, their pupils might have. Among the 43 responses, several trends could be discerned. In agreement with much that was said above, the largest group of teachers (17) were those who suggested that young children would be interested in "concrete attributes" of God: His size, clothing, whether God is a man or a woman, age, location and other factual matters. Almost a third of the teachers (14), however, were able to predict some of the children's actual interests and perplexities reported earlier, including the questions about God's invisibility, omnipresence, moral judgement, causal powers and the like. Seven teachers felt unable to foresee what young children might want to know about God, because "children don't ask about God". It is of some interest to mention that a number of the teachers (5) asked me to disclose what the children actually said that they would like to know about God. When I explicitly asked the teachers whether children of primary school age ever asked any deeper (i.e., philosophical) questions, the majority replied negatively although there was some uncertainty as to what kind of children's questions might be seen as philosophical (e.g., some teachers did not think that asking about the nature of God's causal agency, or how the world began, were philosophical questions).

As we saw in Chapter 3, the majority of children do not know the meaning of religious words encountered in school RE, whether *Amen* or the prayers recited in languages other than English. I therefore asked the teachers to comment on the children's lack of understanding of the *meaning of religious words* and whether the teachers thought that this could be a demotivating factor in children's RE learning. Two distinct patterns of response emerged: The majority of teachers from the schools with Christian RE (17 out of 29) were ready to admit that it was an oversight, indeed failure, not to teach children the meaning of *Amen*. Only in a few instances (4) did the teachers maintain that children did not need to know its meaning and that they themselves still didn't know it, while others stated that they had vaguely assumed that children had already known the meaning of *Amen* or had forgotten it after being introduced to it earlier in the year (5). One of the teachers explained that they didn't teach the meaning of *Amen* because of the presence of children from other faiths in the school. A very different reaction came from the teachers of Hindu, Jewish and Muslim children, who did not see any problem with children's lack of familiarity with the meaning of religious words used in school prayers because, in those traditions, pupils are deliberately taught to memorise prayers or sacred texts first and only later do they begin to dwell on the meanings of those texts and words (cf. Kohn, 2019). In a few instances, teachers from those schools also suggested that some degree of hardship in religious upbringing and formal education is expected and should not be considered demotivating in the long term.

Teachers' statements

T 30: It's not important that they don't know the meaning; it's more important that it goes in, because the sound is so pure, so powerful. And that sound stays with them.

T 31: What they are reciting is God's name. They probably don't understand the concept of that name, but once they grow up … age 16, 17 or 18, they will find out.

T 32: The language of prayer is the language of the heart. Words are not that important to primary children. They will learn them when older.

T 34: It doesn't matter that they don't know the suras; Arabic is like music.

T 43: There is no emphasis on meaning. First, it is memorisation and learning. After that comes translation and understanding the meaning.

I also conveyed to the teachers the children's virtually complete ignorance of the terms "religious education" and "RE". This, however, provoked little surprise among the teachers. A common explanation given by the teachers in the Church of England schools was that the school subjects are not explicitly demarcated for children of primary age ("except for maths, literacy, science, music, and physical education"). According to several teachers in the study, there were additional reasons for non-use of the terms "religious education" or "RE", all of which reflect a certain ambiguity regarding the status of RE within the curriculum. For instance, a number of teachers from those schools mentioned the general unease among some of their colleagues because of having to teach about religion at all, either because of their own lack of religious belief or because of the perceived low status of the subject and even a "stigma" attached to the label (cf. Bastide, 1992; Revell, 2005). By contrast, most teachers from the non-Christian faith schools were confident that children had a good knowledge of what "religious education" refers to albeit in another language (e.g., Deen, Kodesh).

To sum up thus far, in response to my first question to the teachers, namely, their views about young children's conceptual ability for RE, it is clear that the majority of teachers in the study have no expectations of 5- to 7-year-old children to be able to understand the concept of God as the core RE concept nor what relationship between God and any other divine or godly beings might be. The reasons for such low expectations among the teachers were made obvious by the teachers themselves in the next part of the interview described below.

Teachers' perceptions of the usefulness of their training to teach primary RE

Whilst some teachers in the study did not have any training to teach primary RE (e.g., "I trained for secondary teaching, a science subject", T2), the majority unanimously agreed that their teacher training did not prepare them for teaching RE to children of primary school age. Teachers from the Christian background were particularly dissatisfied with their preparation for the role of RE teacher whilst their colleagues from Hindu, Jewish and Muslim schools stated that their solution was to rely on informal input from their respective communities as well as personal experience of growing up within a faith and/or raising their own children as a way of compensating for the lack of adequate formal training.

Teachers' statements

T 4: Very little training. Now that RE is with the core subjects, it's quite worrying. The syllabus that we use is excellent in terms of the content to teach. But in terms of the more abstract concepts, and how children develop those, it isn't really there.

T 5: Can't remember any.

T 13: Very weak ... One short essay on children's thinking and two lectures, and that would be it. One little psychology slot, if that.

T 18: In my training, we were told to give children concrete experiences with artefacts. I feel that's the best approach to take.

T 23: It was a very secular course. I resisted the approach that the PGCE course offered. What is very hard to cope with is that it all boils down to a sickly lowest common denominator that we all belong and we all have birthdays or something ...

T 28: Quite good for a Catholic RE.

T 31: I was helped by the gurus, the temples but there was no psychology ... It would be needed, definitely, to help children understand because they take things literally.

T 34: Never had any formal training how to teach religion. My best training is my own children.

T 38: I rely on what I was taught as a child.

T 44: It was all either common sense or just theories. More subject knowledge would be relevant because I am not religious.

T 45: We did very little RE ... So it's been learning as you go along.

When asked how much information about children's development, that is, psychological research and theory, there was in their training, the teachers in the study conveyed that they either did not have any developmental psychology as part of their training or, if they did, it was dated and mostly irrelevant to their preparation for teaching RE to young children (as opposed to teaching them maths and literacy).

Teachers' statements

T 2: Not very useful ... We talked more about empathy.

T 10: We learned that younger children need concrete experience. They form their experiences on what they are told by their parents.

T 18: I did developmental psychology at the Open University. It's important not to indoctrinate children.

T 21: I had a 3-day course and one session was how children develop but not spiritually. I learn through practice.

T 22: There was less developmental psychology than I would have wanted ... It's more literacy and numeracy based.

T 23: There was nothing about young children's spirituality even though the course was about young children. I would very much welcome that.

T 25: Yes, Piaget ... concrete concepts. Piaget can be useful in my maths teaching but when it comes to spiritual things, I can't see anything useful.

T 27: Piaget was a big feature. Not very useful.

T 28: No, not really. But Piaget was useful. At age 7 you need concrete thinking, it's common sense. It's easy to overestimate what they know.
T 29: A lot of Piaget ... and Vygotsky. Useful to know that children formulate their ideas through talking and until they are verbalising, they are not really thinking. Whereas we adults can think and then verbalise.
T 34: I haven't had enough psychology and want to do it now.
T 36: Yes ... To teach everything from the child's viewpoint.
T 37: All the theories were about language, number, but not children's understanding of religious concepts. But theories don't match my experience; children do understand abstract concepts.
T 43: Psychology module was good but nothing on RE.
T 45: No psychology at all.
T 46: I did A-level psychology, it was relevant.
T 47: It was just a list of stages in children's concepts of God.

Seeing that successful teaching in any subject presupposes some knowledge about where the learners are coming from, i.e., about the pre-existing conceptual foundations, teachers' revelations about the near-complete irrelevance of their professional training for teaching RE to young children are concerning and call for serious attention. For they serve to highlight the urgency of making those courses more relevant to the teachers' task, most of all by including contemporary developmental-psychological research and theory as a basic component of their training.

Teachers' views about the purpose of RE for children of primary school age

During the interviews with the teachers, clear differences emerged regarding the purpose of RE from school to school, reflecting both the official guidance and the teachers' personal views even among and within different Christian schools (cf. Bastide, 1992). Whilst the emphasis on teaching morals as part of RE appears to be strong in all school denominations, the schools differ mostly when it comes to the amount of multi-faith input, especially in the case of younger children (i.e., primary school age). The majority of teachers from Church of England schools said that the main purpose of RE in primary schools should be enhancing children's multi-faith awareness and fostering their social and personal development in order to prepare them for life in a multi-cultural society, as their statements below indicate.

Teachers' statements

T 3: Awareness of different cultures.
T 6: Awareness of other religions in the society and the big questions and how different groups of people answer them.

T 9: To be aware of and appreciate different beliefs and cultures.
T 13: To teach three of the six world religions ... About religion and from religion.
T 14: I like the fact that we teach different religions. Christianity is our focus but we broaden our spectrum to include Judaism and Islam.
T 17: At this school, we teach the three Abrahamic religions and the children are very happy with that. They are able to see the similarities across the religions.
T 19: It's about an understanding between different people with their faiths. We start off by listening to children as people; then we do the three faiths.
T 20: We start off with Christian festivals ... then Judaism and Islam. We need more artefacts.
T 46: To experience all different beliefs and not only Christian and when they are older, they can take whichever belief they believe in.
T 7: Teaching them about people and about themselves ... any puzzling questions in life.
T 16: One of the jobs of RE is to bring out some kind of familiarity between people of different beliefs ... so that they can see that they are very similar.
T 18: At the foundation stage, it's meant to be teaching children about diversity and making them aware that other people think different things ... and showing them lots of pictures and artefacts from different religions. [At this point, I asked the teacher whether the children understood that the teaching was about religion or about God.] No, I don't think they particularly feel it's about the religious element ... It's much better to let their parents introduce it to them.

Only three out of 29 teachers from the schools with Christian RE stated that teaching Christianity ought to be the main purpose of RE, especially when a school had no children from other faiths.

T 1: Ethos of Christianity.
T 2: Christianity as a pleasant idea, the idea of a presence, not solid.
T 26: To introduce them to the person of Jesus and to the liturgical year ... Bible stories, specific prayers.

Further three teachers said that RE should teach children about religion as such:

T 10: To inform children about religion because it exists in our lives; also, to reflect on the meaning of that within their own life.

T 21: To encourage children's spiritual development by teaching them the stories of the faith … stories are full of morals … RE is part of all education.

T 22: First, some basic knowledge of what religion is. Then an awareness of beliefs and morals and what other people think.

In contrast to the majority of RE teachers from predominantly Christian schools, teachers from the other faith schools – Hindu, Jewish and Muslim – held that primary RE should teach the children's respective traditions and a religious identity rather than multi-faith RE.

Teachers' statements

T 33: To teach them the traditions of their people.

T 34: To teach them about their heritage, God's gifts and their responsibilities to God. We don't focus on God in itself but what their religion expects of them.

T 38: Sense of identity – who they are, where they come from.

T 40: Children aged 4 to 7 years should only feel secure and loved. Learning begins at age 7.

It is interesting that none of the 47 teachers in the study expressed the view that God, i.e., this concept, should be at the centre of RE lessons. I mention this in light of young children's overwhelming interest in God, much of it revealed in their own questions about God as we saw in the preceding chapter.

Finally, I asked the teachers whether, in their view, the guidelines for primary RE were adequate. On the whole, they did not think that this was the case citing a number of reasons for such a judgement.

Teachers' statements

T 7: Guidelines are heavily based on Christianity. I would prefer them to be more balanced.

T 8: Too Christian-based to be comfortable. I hope that other faith schools also seek to be broader.

T 11: Too much emphasis on artefacts and places of worship.

T 16: None, when it comes to teaching difficult topics like the crucifixion. It would be helpful to have them.

T 17: We need more [guidance] and what's appropriate for each age. We are not trained how to teach RE as opposed to maths.

Although both the CoRE (2018) and other similar reports acknowledge the shortcomings of primary RE teacher training, there is no mention in any of those publications of the relevance of developmental psychology as a key ingredient in preparing RE teachers for educating young children. A few sources make a general point about the importance of teachers' "understanding the children they are teaching" (e.g., McCreery, 2005, p. 274), but no specific or systematic attempts to bring this about in practice exist. For example, McCreery reported that only one out of 71 trainees for primary RE made the same point. The CoRE report's comments about the state of primary RE teacher training are thus consistent with the findings of the current study, namely, that primary RE "depends heavily on the expertise and enthusiasm of individual teachers" because primary initial training courses "provide very little training about teaching RE" (2018, p. 7). Importantly, however, the Report does not identify the reasons for such deficiencies in the RE teacher training, the most important being the lack of up-to-date information about child development, nor does it mention the need for such information as a basis for designing appropriate primary RE teaching and teacher training programmes.

In short, no hitherto published research and RE literature in general has identified the lack of psychological input in the professional teacher-training courses for primary RE as the main problem affecting primary RE learners and their teachers (e.g., McCreery, 2005; Revell, 2005). Rather, RE literature is replete with claims that before 7 years of age children's concepts in general are concrete rather than abstract, including their concept of God (e.g., Erricker, 2011b, p. 65). Such claims are the basis for recommendation that the key concepts for children to grasp in the foundation stage and first year of school should be those that immediately relate to their experience of "belonging, celebrating and specialness" (Erricker, 2011c, p. 107). Yet, as I argued earlier in the book, none of the authors advocating such a strategy for primary RE can cite any evidence which demonstrates that young children's concept of God does not relate to their experience. In Chapter 4, we saw that 5- to 7-year-old children rely primarily or solely on their own experience of the physical world when inferring that God is its cause, as evidenced by their performance in the natural-theological reasoning test, where children commonly justify their judgements about natural objects by citing their experiences of seeing or handling them and understanding their causal characteristics and origins. Extant evidence further shows that, in this respect, children are no different from adults (for a review, see Petrovich, 2019).

Teachers' statements regarding the issues addressed in their interviews illustrate a marked discrepancy between the teachers' perceptions of children's conceptual abilities and interests, on the one hand, and children's abilities revealed in their performance in several parts of the current study as well as in the wider developmental research and theory, on the other. The discrepancy seems to be a consequence of two related factors. First, the paucity of directly relevant psychological research designed to establish what young children understand about God (or religion) before receiving formal RE. The second factor is a consequence of the first, namely, deficiencies in the currently existing RE teacher training programmes for primary schools. The identified discrepancy is substantial and goes a long way towards explaining why many of the children's own questions about God remain unaddressed in school RE. Yet it is of utmost importance that children's education, in this case RE, should be structured around their existing conceptual needs and interests so that it can make a genuine contribution to children's overall education and development. The best way of resolving the existing discrepancies is through direct research with young children, which should be planned to address specific questions pertaining to primary age, and whose research findings can then be used as a basis for designing teacher training programmes of direct and specific relevance to primary RE.

Note

1 In the previous chapter, I mentioned that a number of children, especially younger, from all school denominations seemed to experience some confusion about such relationships even when not stating them in crudely anthropomorphic terms.

Chapter 7

Religious understanding in the early years: What can RE learn from young children?

In this short chapter, I seek to provide a psychological account of young children's conceptual abilities needed for understanding RE content and the effect of school-based RE on their understanding of, and interest in, the subject. In light of substantial psychological evidence that children do not approach any domain of formal learning *tabula rasa* but do so with some already acquired foundational concepts specific to a domain (Wellman & S. Gelman, 1998), teaching young children in any subject ought to build on their already existing concepts and theories belonging in that domain. Developmental research shows that forging such links between existing and novel concepts can ensure deeper and longer-lasting connections between the ideas that emerge in everyday reasoning, on the one hand, and in formal educational settings, on the other (Kikas, 1998). Accordingly, I suggested earlier in the book that there are no valid conceptual or educational reasons for treating RE as an exception to this general finding about cognitive development. In the case of the religious domain, it is thus safe to assume that children start learning about it by building on some already existing concepts of a religious kind, notably the concept of God as a causal agent (Petrovich, 2019). Yet, according to many in the RE field, the purpose of RE is unclear because it lacks a core concept around which to structure RE teaching in a "modern democratic society" where "the value of religion, or God in particular" is perceived as divisive (e.g., Erricker, 2011a, p. 8). Such concerns, needless to say, are not motivated by what research has found to be the case with children's understanding of the world around them but by broader societal issues that are of no immediate or direct relevance to young children's understanding of God. As the preceding chapters in this volume have shown, young children do think about God and many are keen to talk about God (cf. Takriti, Barrett & Barrow, 2006; Sorea & Scarneci-Domnisoru, 2018), occasionally asking me during the testing what I thought about the issues implied by the questions. Even the children who expressed a lack of interest in learning further about God were able to give coherent reasons for not having a question of interest about God. In a nutshell, therefore, one

DOI: 10.4324/9781003004639-7

major lesson for RE to learn from young children is that God should be at the centre of primary RE as its key topic.

Further, data in the current study strongly contradict the assumption among many RE specialists that young children are interested in cultural differences among individuals belonging to different faiths. This assumption underpins the stipulation that RE should "help children mature in relation to their own patterns of belief and behaviour through exploring religious beliefs and practices and related human experiences found in major world faiths" (Read et al., 1992, cited in Lowndes, 2011a, p. 23). In the same vein, RE should teach children to "juxtapose the 'content' of religious life-worlds of adherents with the 'content' of the pupils' life-worlds" and thereby "become informed about religious beliefs and values and are able to use them as instruments for the critical evaluation of their own beliefs and values" (Grimmitt, 1987, cited in Lowndes, 2011a, p. 23). Jackson (2000) similarly advocates that pupils aged 5 to 7 years ought to engage with "Actions, objects and technical terms identified from the pages of the story books" that are found in different religious cultures and thereby create "bridges" between "pupils' experience of life" and "the experience of the children introduced in the story" (p. 138). In light of the evidence reported in the current book, which was obtained from children in the same age range as above, such proposals seem far removed from children's actual religious interests, namely, the being of God. Put simply, it is difficult to see how young children's learning about the customs and traditions of the cultures encountered in school RE can help them create links between the experiences described in a story, on one hand, and children's own experience "of life", on the other, while still being able to answer their questions about God. A 7-year-old spoke for the majority of the 431 children in the current study when explaining why he did not have a question of interest about God: "I am interested in some bits but not all … I'm not really interested in … like … twelve gods in each country and things like that". He then added that he would "really like to know how God makes stuff just by thinking about it". In short, data from 5 to 7 years old children reported in the volume demonstrate that their religious interests are not anthropological or cultural, as sometimes suggested (e.g., Jackson, 1990), but are often metaphysical, shared also by scientists, philosophers, theologians as well as lay adults. Linking RE with science, including evolution, would thus be beneficial not just for secondary (Reiss, 2009), but primary school pupils, too, because of the evidence that 5- to 7-year-olds reflect on the links between the two domains (Madge, 1965). For example, although Madge undertook to investigate "the interests and *religious* (my emphasis) conceptions of children in the primary school years", she discovered in the course of the study that children's spontaneous interests of a religious kind were "clearly associated with scientific ideas" (p. 7), often presenting as a "search for causes" (p. 13).

The multi-faith conception of RE is also grounded in the assumption that concepts in general, including religious, are transmitted by others and learned from others rather than children themselves playing an active role in their acquisition. For instance, a number of studies maintain that children acquire a concept of God and religiosity (spirituality) as a consequence of learning in the home and at school (e.g., Heland-Kurzak, 2019; De Roos, Iedema & Miedema, 2001; Wenger, 2001). Those studies however, do not control for the alternative possibility, namely, that some religious concepts may emerge in development without any tutoring or input from others as, indeed, many of our early or foundational concepts emerge. This is not to say that children's initial concepts are not influenced by the linguistic expressions and ideas to which they are exposed within their religious communities and which they employ when answering questions such as "who is God?" or "where does God live?" and similar. They certainly are, as much of the extant evidence suggests. Crucially, however, results from such studies do not establish that children would not have formed a concept of God without the influence of their own religious culture, not least because of considerable psychological evidence documenting that basic or foundational concepts precede language acquisition (e.g., Mandler, 2004).

Wenger (2001) went even further in his argument that cultural influences have a causal role in the acquisition of religious concepts when stating that only children raised in religious environments "might develop theory-like understanding around the concept of God and God's activities" (p. 41). This is manifestly not the case based on young children's responses described in this book: Children aged 5 to 7 years do not depend on "religious environments" to understand the world in causal terms and postulate God as its cause. It is pertinent to point out that Wenger did not have a control group consisting of children without any religious involvement (i.e., from a secular culture), which would be necessary to support his thesis that understanding God in abstract terms is not possible without RE teaching. It is therefore arguable that Wenger's data for all age groups are best explained in terms of language acquisition (i.e., religious vocabulary) rather than in terms of a spontaneously constructed "theory", as this term is used in developmental psychology (e.g., Keil, 2006; Wellman & S. Gelman, 1992). Wenger indeed acknowledges that his findings are in agreement with Elkind (1964) and Nye and Carlson (1984) as well as Piaget, all of whom argued for a concrete-to-abstract developmental shift in children's understanding of the concept of God.

The studies mentioned above are representative of the publications in RE journals which address young children's allegedly limited cognitive capacity to acquire and use appropriately an abstract concept of God. By contrast, evidence in this volume suggests that 5- to 7-year-old children come to school with such a concept already in place and that hence RE does not play a formative role in its acquisition, that is, in young children's understanding of God's fundamental characteristics – ontological as well as causal. With such a concept already present in their conceptual inventory, one of the main initial tasks of school-based RE is to reinforce children's existing understanding of God and provide meaningful links with other religious concepts, chiefly by enriching their vocabulary specific to religion and thereby enabling them to establish meaningful connections between and among different religious constructs. In his plea for a universal RE provision, Schweitzer (2005) invoked children's legal and social rights to religious education by making a particularly important point that "children's right to religion should be understood in educational terms in the first place" (p. 107). Although Schweitzer does not address school-based RE specifically, nor any particular age during childhood, his educational perspective is fundamentally correct and applicable to even the youngest children. Thus his argument that, although younger children cannot speak for themselves in this matter, adults need to make an effort to find out more about children's needs and "be prepared to accept that even young people might have something meaningful to contribute to their own religious development and education" (Schweitzer, 2005, pp. 106–107). Whilst not citing any psychological research or theories in his paper, Schweitzer's argument is consistent with the general point made in this book, i.e., that children's cognitive needs ought to be a primary concern in an educational setting. His point, needless to emphasise, is also consistent with the evidence reported in the current book which shows that even 5-year-olds are able to say what views and questions they have about God and many other issues encompassed by RE.

Contrary to the anxieties expressed by some RE specialists and by the opponents of RE in general, a truly educational RE is unlikely to become a mechanism for stifling children's autonomy and independence of thought (e.g., Marples, cited in Erricker 2011a, p. 11) or serve as a vehicle for indoctrination of children. Evidence obtained from children in the current study suggests that neither faith schools nor RE as such stifle children's readiness to question the information received when given opportunities to do so. In the case of very young children, whose vocabulary is limited and who lack the skills needed for initiating questioning and participating in arguments, such opportunities can be created by using methods that are designed to elicit directly relevant responses. Several decades of sustained methodological effort in developmental research have made it possible for researchers to obtain relevant data even from preverbal children, such as by using targeted questioning under the conditions that require minimal or no verbal responding.

Whilst Lowndes (2011a) answers well the question about what counts as good RE, namely, "Good RE happens when it is child-centred and child-driven and when it deals with concepts that are of interest to children and that resonate with their lives" (p. 32), she overlooks the fact that the "child-centred" approach depends in practice on what educators know about the child in order to be able to "centre" their educational efforts appropriately. We saw in Chapter 6 that the majority of teachers admit that they do not know enough about young children's thinking. As already pointed out, this is not surprising because developmental psychology is not a component on PGCE training courses and nor is psychological research mentioned in the educational literature. Consequently, RE teachers have no access to information about young children's abilities and learning potential in this domain that would allow them to centre their teaching on children's conceptual needs. For this reason, primary RE can be more accurately described as adult-centred and adult-driven, focused on meeting the needs and goals of different groups of adults, whose main concern is either to prepare children for life in a modern multi-cultural and multi-faith society or bolster their cultural identity. In that vein, Lowndes (2011a) provides a list of parental expectations of RE and highlights the effort made by schools to "provide pupils with a range of religious beliefs and practices to investigate across the primary phase" (p. 24). Waddup (1992) similarly contends that the aims of RE in infant school are distinctly social and cultural, characterised by the "life themes" approach that was originally proposed by Goldman. As already mentioned, such social and cultural motives for RE provision do not aim to respond specifically and primarily to children's conceptual needs but to satisfy adults' cultural and social expectations. Thus, for example, the "life-themes" approach seeks to familiarise children with diverse cultural events and artefacts while mentioning "God as creator" as just one of the 27 "main elements" of RE for young children (e.g., Waddup, 1992, p. 38). Needless to say, RE conceived as a study of diverse religious beliefs and traditions does not make it sufficiently clear to children of primary age what the beliefs are about. Consequently, as we saw in Chapter 3, children fail to make connections between RE stories and other RE content, on the one hand, and God, on the other, because such connections are not explicitly forged and/or encouraged in formal RE lessons. It is also pertinent to point out that research with children as well as adults suggests that some forms of cultural religious input actually impart anthropomorphic representations of deity in adults (e.g., Barrett & Van Orman, 1996; Petrovich, 2019). As well as this, certain RE content appears to augment children's difficulties in grasping the relationship between God, on the one hand, and the salient figures in a given faith tradition, on the other. Although such patterns can be found among children from all the traditions included in the study, for obvious reasons the confusions are most frequent among children receiving Christian RE.

- I don't know how they are connected [God & Jesus] (age 5).
- Jesus died to save us and God just died (age 5).
- [What does it mean to be a prophet?] A God (age 5).
- Jesus is God's dad. [Who is Jesus' dad?] I don't know (age 6).
- God is stuck on the cross all the time and Jesus is teaching people about God (age 6).
- [What is the connection between God and Jesus?] I'm not sure about that one (age 7).

- They both [God & Jesus] have a legend story how they died and how God created the world (age 7).
- He [Mohammed] is the last God to be made but he is dead now (age 7).
- I want to know who is the prophet and who is God (age 7).

Although the examples cited above highlight some of the challenges that young children face in RE, there is also evidence of young children's ability to recognise them as conceptually challenging. We saw in Chapter 3 that children aged between 5 and 7 years appear to show good metacognitive insight when pinpointing the reasons for not understanding the RE content in question, such as not knowing the meaning of the words encountered in that content. For those reasons, children's actual understanding of God is most clearly revealed in their everyday reasoning about the world, such as when pondering the origin of natural entities and, also, when arriving at their own questions about God. Children's God, according to the majority of those data, is certainly not a physically anthropomorphic agent but one whose intuited nature they struggle to convey by employing analogies, metaphors and other non-literal devices. Yet, many adults, lay as well as specialists, are sceptical that thinking about the world can lead children to conceptualise God. Bates (1992), for example, casts doubt on the connection between reasoning about the natural world and God "as [not] having anything necessarily to do with RE at all" (p. 102). Notwithstanding Bates's assertion, evidence from children described in Chapter 4 of this volume documents the strength as well as validity of such a connection in human thought already in early childhood and across different cultures.

Pace Erricker's attempt to make "a case for why RE should have a multicultural or pluralistic approach" (2011a, p. 17), it is not clear how this could be accomplished while simultaneously meeting young children's conceptual needs and interests that they are able to articulate and which, overwhelmingly, focus on God. Erricker's related claim, that RE "needs to be about how we make sense of the world and our place in it" (p. 57), can be answered by extant psychological evidence that both children and adults "make sense of the world" by observing it, forming hypotheses about its structure and origin, postulating causes of its different components and constructing theories about its manifold aspects (Petrovich, 2019).

In the concluding chapter, I will attempt to address the question how primary school-based RE may be able to fulfil its educational purpose by taking account of the evidence obtained in the current study as well as developmental research more broadly.

Chapter 8

Conclusion

Taking account of the main findings in the current study, and of contemporary child development research and theory, implications for an RE appropriate for children aged 5 to 7 years can be drawn out. To begin with, a truly educational RE needs to meet children's cognitive needs and capacities that are specific to RE and which cannot be met by any other school subject. Research findings reported in this book indicate that this should include, primarily, children's overriding interest in the concept of God (i.e., the nature of such a being). Curiosity about God and God's attributes is an issue that persists in all age groups, including adults (e.g., Fontana, 1971), and hence should be at the centre of school-based RE. Yet, this very concept is absent from many primary RE syllabuses on the assumption that it is too difficult for young children and should thus only be approached indirectly. The most obvious problem with this advice is that it is not backed by any purposely obtained empirical evidence.

In spite of the differences in the content of school-based RE among the denominations represented in this project, evidence reported in the book indicates that what is common to children from the different schools is fundamentally conceptual. The most salient common finding in the study is that children's reasoning about God occurs reliably in the context of their thinking about the natural world. In other words, children from diverse religious backgrounds ask the same basic questions about the world and God and answer them in highly similar ways. However, as we saw from the children's RE interviews, school-based RE as presently conceived does not seem to address those issues consistently nor in sufficient depth but, in many cases, focuses on teaching children about the variety of cultural expressions of religious beliefs or, in other cases, seeks to build children's sense of belonging to a particular religious community.

Evidence obtained from 47 RE teachers is equally informative and highlights a marked discrepancy between the teachers' perceptions of children's abilities to understand abstract concepts, on the one hand, and children's actual understanding of abstract concepts addressed in the current study, on the other. Teachers' experiences of attending professional training

DOI: 10.4324/9781003004639-8

courses indicate that such discrepancies in the RE theory and practice can only be overcome by amending those courses so that they include a substantial component of contemporary developmental psychology. The lack of psychological input in teacher-training courses has greater consequences for children's RE learning than that in most other subjects because it is less obvious to the teacher how children reason in the RE domain than it is when teaching them in their other subjects where tangible and often instant feedback about children's progress is possible (e.g., literacy, maths, science).

The RE teachers expressed a few other concerns affecting RE, notably insufficient time allocated to the subject as a major obstacle to achieving its better reception among young children. As a teacher from a Church of England school explained, the RE time slot allows the teacher to read a story (e.g., Noah's Ark), then ask the children to draw the content of the story (e.g., a few animals), but no time in which to address the meaning of the story, i.e., the topic of redemption. The perceived lack of parental support for RE has also been cited as an obstacle to teaching it effectively in some schools because, sometimes, parental preferences for faith schools are motivated by academic rather than religious reasons.

Cognitive-developmental case for primary RE

Over the years, there have been many arguments against teaching RE to children aged between 3 and 8 years and hence also against primary RE teacher training (e.g., Bastide, 1980). Findings reported and discussed in this book contradict the general argument against RE for a number of reasons, one of which being its proponents' reliance on Goldman's (1960) findings that Biblical teaching is of no benefit to young children but in fact can be harmful. Children's statements presented in Chapter 3 of this volume speak otherwise: 5- to 7-year-olds frequently conveyed that they enjoy listening to Bible stories but do not understand their content so as to be able to reproduce it later because, as they made it clear, they do not understand the meanings of the words used in the stories and hence find them difficult to recall and find RE as such to be hard. Goldman's use of Bible stories to investigate children's capacity for non-literal understanding of religious terms would certainly merit replication by developmental psychologists, mainly because children's understanding of similar conceptual relations to those contained in Biblical passages (e.g., metaphors, analogies) has been successfully studied and documented in other domains of their reasoning (e.g., Goswami, 1992; Vosniadou & Ortony, 1983). The suggestion that RE should focus on teaching the religious language used in its lessons (Bates, 1992) is quite consistent with the findings described in this book and merits further empirical research. Above all, the current study is in agreement with those scholars who have argued that RE for young children should include discussion of the nature of God because it is a topic of interest among adult students, too (Fontana, 1971). Similar observations about adults' interest in God, yet their frequently expressed experiences of feeling deprived of opportunities to discuss their understanding of God, were noted by other authors (e.g., Fowler, 1986; Petrovich, 2019).

The educational advantages of addressing the concept of God through formal education are numerous, not least on account of its potential to enhance children's inquisitiveness about similarly abstract conceptual issues in other knowledge domains, including scientific (e.g., of unobservable entities). Further, learning about God would help young children acquire the criteria needed for evaluating abstract concepts in general and ultimately enable them to become balanced in their acceptance of the differences involved in handling such a concept. In short, educating children to differentiate between matters of faith (i.e., beliefs as mental states), on the one hand, and the manifold cultural expressions of those states, on the other, can bring children significantly closer to becoming religiously educated citizens in due course.

In light of the evidence obtained from participants in the current study, it is clear that RE teaching in primary schools should not be a matter of choice from among "six different schools of thought in RE" (Blaylock, 2004, p. 13) but, rather, ought to be evidence-based, that is, guided by the findings of systematic and targeted research with young children. This is still not the case, however, despite a long-standing plea that "the teaching of religion needs to be based far more firmly on relevant research" (Burt, 1971, p. 10). Burt was also right to argue that our understanding of God, i.e., concepts of such a being, "is plainly one for the psychologist" to investigate (p. 7) and lamented the non-involvement of academic psychology in this area of children's education. Yet, perhaps not surprisingly given the lack of the relevant psychological research at the time of his writing, Burt too doubted that younger children had an abstract concept of God on which to build their learning in school RE. A decade later, Cox (1983) similarly called for investigation of young children's apparent conceptual difficulties in RE as "urgently needed" (p. 37), but little has changed. A silver lining in the delay could be in the fact that "relevant research" stands a better chance of being carried out now, after several decades of flourishing methodological innovations and theoretical advances that have occurred in all areas of psychology, including developmental.

Relevance of psychological research to primary RE

My general point in this book has been that the case for RE in primary schools ought to be made on the same grounds as that for the other academic subjects, i.e., conceptual. This means that purposely obtained evidence about children's cognitive needs specific to religion, which could not be met by any other school subject, must be given priority when considering

RE teaching policy. Goldman's emphasis on children's emotions as a guide for teaching primary RE, which is still adhered to, gives a distorted picture of children's overall mental capacities in that it overlooks their capacity for rational thought about invisible and other abstract entities (e.g., S. Gelman, 2004; S. Gelman & Wellman, 1991; Estes, Wellman & Woolley, 1989). Children's emotional needs, however important, cannot be a realistic basis for designing syllabuses in any school subject but are addressed by professional bodies established for the purpose of caring for children's emotional wellbeing.

Seeing that children acquire a concept of God before they start school, the question of interest to developmental psychology is how early this occurs. Difficulties of studying experimentally abstract concepts in pre-verbal or young pre-school children present significant methodological challenges to answering such a question. Nevertheless, some important successes have been achieved in the research on early understanding of numerical, spatial and other abstract concepts in pre-verbal children (e.g., Mandler, 2004; Mandler & McDonough, 1993), which makes it more likely that religious abstract concepts too may become amenable to controlled and systematic study at some point in the future.

The relevance of employing appropriate methods in this area of research may be illustrated by considering research outcomes of the studies where the standards of psychological research were not fully implemented. For example, in her intriguing paper on young children's theological understanding, Frady (2019) explored "how 2-year old children expressed theological ideas" (p. 185) by engaging them in "Godly play". The procedure makes use of a "Bible story box" (p. 188) filled with figurines representing the story of Jesus and the children from the Gospel of Mark 10, 13–16. Twenty children aged 2.1 to 2.11 years who attended "faith-based early centres of evangelical tradition" in the southern USA listened to the story being read to them while simultaneously playing with the items from the box. After hearing the story, children had a choice of either hearing the story again or playing with the story items for about 15 minutes (p. 189). On the basis of children's behaviour during the play session, described as "Eager Receptiveness to attentively listen to and focus on a Bible story that was told" (p. 195), Frady concluded that 2-year-olds from Christian centres "when approached with the developmentally appropriate method of Godly Play, render, co-create, and become joint theologians with the researcher" (p. 195). What detracts from Frady's conclusion that children's response to the story is of theological significance is the fact that there was no control group or other control variables to ensure that children did not just simply enjoy the sound of the story teller's voice, or any other aspect of the situation, rather than the *theological content* of the story. For it is possible that *any* story read to this group of 2-year-olds could have elicited the same behaviour in the presence of the same toys. It should be said that the absence of such controls in Frady's method in no way rules out the possibility that very young children may have a capacity for religious cognition that emerges early in development and/or is innately pre-specified. Innateness of learning mechanisms that drive cognitive development is a mainstream idea in developmental psychology (e.g., Baillargeon, 2008; Elman et al., 1996; Spelke, 2000), and some of those mechanisms may be pre-disposed for the acquisition of highly abstract concepts, including that of God (Petrovich, 2019). In Frady's study, however, alternative interpretations are equally possible.

Problems with child-centred RE and its agreed syllabuses

In the previous chapter, I argued that the "child-centred" approach to RE teaching has never existed in either theory or practice of RE for one obvious reason: Child-centred approach presupposes a reliable and valid understanding of children's cognitive needs and capacities on which to base educational interventions. This has never been the case in the field of RE because no psychological research has hitherto documented the state of children's conceptual prerequisites for RE. Thus, although the child-centred approach advocated by the Plowden Report (1967) was to be "psychologically informed" (Kay, 2002, p. 204), the child psychology that the Report had in mind was about children's emotional rather than cognitive needs. All subsequent versions of "child-centred" approach similarly focus on children's emotional and social development rather than conceptual (e.g., Hull, 2000; Lowndes, 2011a; Waddup, 1992).

The notion of "the agreed syllabus" as a basis for RE is also problematic in that it often serves the needs of adults rather than children. As I pointed out earlier in the volume, to contend that an agreed syllabus is "the product of a democratic process involving religious groups, teachers and local authority representatives" and that therefore "*ought* to be satisfactory" (Kay, 2002), fails to meet this very expectation because it takes no account of young children's conceptual needs and interests. In other words, there is nothing in the mechanism of reaching an agreement between different adults' ideals and goals that guarantees its usefulness when it comes to furthering young children's understanding of core conceptual issues in religion. Evidence from both children and teachers reported in this book does indeed demonstrate that adults have little awareness of young children's capacity to acquire and handle abstract concepts. Adults' own recollections of processing childhood RE cannot be a reliable guide either because of what is known about the nature of human memory and its development across life span (e.g., Bauer & Wewerka, 1995; Bauer, Larkina, Gúler, & Burch, 2019). Hence neither "child-centred" nor "agreed syllabus" frameworks can provide a route to an educationally valid primary RE unless they are based on, and backed up by, directly relevant empirical evidence obtained through research with young children.

To summarise, the discrepancy between children's actual cognitive abilities and conceptual interests, on the one hand, and their teachers' lack of awareness of those abilities, on the other, is one of the most pressing problems in primary RE. Put simply, teachers are expected to approach primary RE in the same way as they do secondary RE and the main question in practice is how to transmit its content in the right doses. The main drawbacks of such an approach, as already pointed out, are that (a) it doesn't take account of young children's cognitive abilities, and (b) it assumes that young children are interested in multi-faith RE content or other cultural information of a religious kind. In Chapter 3, we saw that young children' inability to make connections between various religious themes (e.g., festivals) and God, that is, understand what makes them religious, is a direct consequence of not receiving appropriate instruction about the meaning of the stories and religious words encountered in RE. Providing young children with meaningful connections is necessary because the events in RE stories are not a part of their everyday experience of the world but a form of cultural input and, as such, require educational help in order to enable them to assimilate their meaning. This, however, is not what primary RE teachers are trained for or expected to do because of the pervasive assumption within RE that children of primary age lack the ability to understand abstract concepts whereas they are likely to remember some other aspects of their RE experience (e.g., emotions triggered by stories, religious artefacts, chanting).

RE teacher-training challenges

The inadequacy of primary RE teacher training was made clear by all 47 teachers in the study. Absence of contemporary developmental psychology from their professional training is, undoubtedly, a major cause of the teachers' uncertainty regarding the right approach when teaching RE to children aged between 5 and 7 years. Publications in RE journals either do not mention the relevance of psychological research or cite a few dated sources; instead, trainee teachers are encouraged to engage in reflecting on their own feelings about teaching religious education to children of primary age, including paying attention to the feelings about their own childhood experiences of religion as a guide to their practice, whilst also acknowledging that many teachers of RE are non-believers (e.g., McCreery, 2005). Thus, as we saw earlier, Gay's (2002) argument that RE should also be about teachers' "understanding the children they are teaching" received only one trainee teacher's endorsement in a group of 71 (McCreery, 2005, p. 274). In another study that deals with primary RE teacher training, Revell (2005) found that school-based RE teacher training is no better than that offered on PGCE courses, particularly when it comes to opportunities to observe RE lessons, which are few and far between. In short, the studies mentioned above illustrate the problem highlighted earlier, namely, that primary RE focuses on the teachers and the likely impact of their personal religious history on their teaching of young children rather than on children's conceptual involvement with RE content. The assumption that teachers' own childhood experiences can be a reliable guide to their teaching of young children is unwarranted given the psychological evidence about memory development and childhood amnesia (e.g., Bauer et al., 2019). In other words, teachers' recollections of their own religious history and the influences that have led to their current beliefs may be misleading in this respect as they can bias teachers in the wrong direction. In contrast to this "personal history" approach to RE teaching, Mitchell (1980) argued that school RE should have an "academic aim" rather than be concerned "with the individual's search for a 'faith to live by' or with society's concern to hand on a living religious tradition" (p. 133). He also argued that RE as an academic subject should be compulsory because it provides "an understanding of the meaning and purpose of life", thereby giving unity to the entire educational process (Mitchell, 1980, p. 134). As I have already tried to suggest, from the viewpoint of developmental psychology and the needs of very young children, there are even more basic reasons for making RE a compulsory component of every child's education, namely, its singular potential to answer children's questions of a religious or theological import, notably those about God, that no other school subject is expected to do.

A peculiar feature of RE as a school subject, compared to the other subjects, seems to be its explicit acceptance that the subject can be taught by teachers who may not have any interest in religion. Of the 47 RE teachers in the current sample, I encountered two who were in that position. On the basis of the teachers' responses to the questions asked in the interview, it wasn't possible to ascertain the reasons for those teachers' views and whether they saw RE as having no educational value. If so, this would suggest that RE differs radically from the other school subjects regarding its potential to inspire interest in its students; for it would hardly be acceptable to consider entrusting the teaching of mathematics, science, language or, indeed, any other learning domain to teachers who take the view that any of those subjects lacks intrinsic educational value. Nor is there a parallel expectation that teachers in the other school subjects might be influenced by their personal history to the extent that it affects their teaching. In view of such concerns, it is arguable that RE, like any other school subject, should merit a place on the curriculum only if it can be seen as capable of advancing children's cognitive growth and contributing to their knowledge in this particular domain. It follows that, contrary to the recommendations that pupils in early years RE should engage with concepts such as "remembering, celebration, belonging or special" (Lowndes, 2011b, p. 140), the focus should instead be on core religious concepts, in accordance with young children's documented conceptual needs and interests. Put simply, for RE to be beneficial in the long term, its aim should be to support rather than thwart children's early interest in the subject. As Millais's 1864 painting "*My second sermon*" shown below aptly illustrates, loss of interest in

Figure 8.1 Millais's 1864 painting "My second sermon" © Guildhall Art Gallery (City of London Corporation).

religion, broadly speaking, is an all too frequent long-term outcome of childhood RE, formal or informal. Its counterpart, Millais's 1863 painting on the front cover of this book depicts the same child's initial state of vivid expectation at the prospect of learning or experiencing something new while listening to her first sermon (Figure 8.1).

How can psychological research contribute to primary RE?

My argument for a greater role of developmental psychology in teacher training courses implies, admittedly, that changes within psychology are also needed. The reasons for its complete absence from the field of RE are manifold but some that are pertinent to this argument have been mentioned by other authors. Matthews (1984), for example, points out that, "developmental psychologists are much more likely to concern themselves with the development of capacities that are widely prized in our society than with the development of a capacity that is generally ignored" (p. 116). Indeed, the sheer volume of psychological research on children's scientific (e.g., biology, physics, psychology) and mathematical understanding, compared to their understanding of metaphysical, including theological, ideas is sufficient to corroborate Matthews's judgement. The availability of research funding for the former, compared to the latter, topics speaks volumes about the discrepancy between the two streams of psychological research effort in terms of both quantity and quality. All this is mirrored in the academic teaching of psychology which, needless to elaborate, is vastly better supported and offering greater opportunities for further study in the areas of research and teaching dealing with scientific and mathematical development than in the areas that involve children's metaphysical and theological understanding.

In brief, deficiencies within the academic education of psychologists, which fails to prepare them for research in the domain of religious cognition, can explain, to a large extent, psychology's non-involvement in the field of religious education. Psychology graduates generally have little background knowledge of the philosophical underpinnings of religious cognition or even of the interface between religious and scientific questions that run through the history of human thought. Without some knowledge of this background, it is hardly possible to come up with fruitful and researchable hypotheses about religious understanding and its development. Yet, all this could change in a relatively short time, chiefly by designing degree programmes for psychologists with a carefully planned added component that involves religion, broadly speaking (e.g., philosophy of religion), which would enable them to generate ideas suitable for research by psychological methods and across life span.

In the final part of this chapter, I venture to suggest a tentative practical proposal on how school-based primary RE might fulfil its main educational role of advancing children's cognitive development in the domain of religious understanding while at the same time managing to retain their interest in the subject.

As a developmental psychologist, I see the advantages in differentiating between two kinds of RE content: *foundational* and *denominational.* Foundational RE deals with children's basic conceptual questions of a religious kind, such as those that they ask about God, and treats them as distinct from the cultural, i.e., denominational, answers to some of those basic questions.[1] Foundational RE can also provide children with a framework for coordinating learning about science and religion, not least because both science and religion deal with some of the same basic conceptual issues and share a number of metaphysical concerns with which even preschoolers are familiar (e.g., existence of different kinds of unobservable entities, nature of causality). At present, however, many RE practitioners see the two areas of education – scientific and religious – as radically different in the sense that scientific education relies on "children's understanding about the world" and makes use of a "conceptual enquiry approach", whilst implying that this is not the case with religious education (Bellchambers, 2011, p. 165). The assumption that children's everyday experience of the world is not directly relevant to RE, especially to their concepts of God, underpins the advice to primary teachers that they should teach RE by feeling their way through as they go along rather than focusing on core religious concepts. For example, in their chapter titled "What next for RE and the primary curriculum?", Erricker and Bellchambers (2011) list a number of issues relevant to 5-year-olds, none of which is explicitly religious or theological but all focus on humanity and its diverse challenges, including climate change and sustainability, quality of life and wellbeing, the cyborg and body perfect as well as "religious and non-religious tensions" (pp. 202–208). Yet, children's performance in the natural-theological test described in Chapter 4 documents a key role that children's everyday experience of the physical world plays in their reasoning about God.

Foundational RE can thus make a unique contribution to children's education because it addresses those conceptual questions specific to religion that children begin to raise before starting school, such as those pertaining to the origin of the natural world, the nature of divinity, God's moral agency, mind-body distinction, beginning and end of life and the like, many of which children in the current study articulated as their most important questions about God (Chapter 5). Put simply, the main emphasis in foundational RE ought to be on the conceptual legitimacy of the questions central to religion rather than on the cultural-historical variety of the answers to those questions. The uniqueness of religious questions and issues is sufficient to motivate further study of religion and also withstand attempts to reduce it to other forms of study (e.g., anthropology or ethnography). Last, but not least, foundational RE could add the necessary rigour to the subject and thus be truly educational while at the same time avoiding ideological controversy. In a word, children's ability to raise and understand issues inherent in religion, as documented in this book, should be sufficient to warrant adequate RE provision in schools on the grounds that it can make a distinctive contribution to children's cognitive development.

It is important to stress that none of the arguments for the primacy of foundational RE at primary school age precludes the teaching of particular faiths (i.e., denominational RE) as well. For instance, denominational RE content can provide suitable illustrations of the points made in foundational RE. In the current RE practice, however, the choice of particular doctrines for inclusion in school-based RE is typically determined by factors other than children's cognitive-psychological development and as such lacks a universal dimension that psychologists seek to identify and explain its development. Put simply, by virtue of addressing conceptual issues inherent in religion as such, the foundational component of RE constitutes its starting point. In contrast, denominational RE, which is not concerned solely or primarily with children's cognition, is more likely to involve children's emotional and social tendencies by teaching them specific behaviours and seeking to enhance their awareness of belonging to social groups with a shared identity. Consequently, the two forms of RE ought to be seen as performing distinct rather than alternative roles.

I have argued throughout this book that young children's school-based religious education ought to be guided by reliable psychological research. This is especially important when it comes to primary schools where young children's verbal and communication skills are typically insufficient to enable RE teachers to ascertain children's actual conceptual engagement with the subject. In light of considerable evidence that young children do engage in untutored or everyday religious thought, such a developmental tendency merits educational support in the same way that their everyday or informal scientific thought does.

To transform primary RE theory and practice, it is essential that psychologists, developmental and educational, join the debate about school-based RE. Because psychological research is at present not taken into account when designing RE syllabuses, the most important reason for keeping RE on the curriculum, namely, its potential to meet pupils' specific cognitive needs, is being overshadowed by secondary issues such as how many of the religious traditions to include, how much to teach about each and the like. Although many practical questions may need to be addressed before an implementation of the two-component RE – foundational and denominational – becomes possible, such questions are technicalities and ought not to detract from the cognitive-psychological rationale for maintaining the presence of RE in primary schools.

Note

1 Attfield's (1984) term "religious foundations" (p. 8) is similar to "foundational RE" in its emphasis on a focused or "explicit" approach to primary RE, where the focus is on God. Attfield's connotation of "foundational" is different in the sense that it refers to the fundamentals of Christianity rather than conceptual foundations as this term is used in developmental psychology.

References

Amsel, E., Klaczynski, P. A., Johnston, A., Bench, S., Close, J., Sadler, E. & Walker, R. (2008). A dual-process account of the development of scientific reasoning: The nature and development of metacognitive intercession skills. *Cognitive Development, 23*, 452–471.

Attfield, D. G. (1984). Implicit religion. *British Journal of Religious Education, 7* (1), 8–13.

Baillargeon, R. (2008). Innate ideas revisited: For a principle of persistence in infants' physical reasoning. *Perspectives on Psychological Science, 3* (1), 2–13.

Barrett, J. L. (2000). Exploring the natural foundations of religion. *Trends in Cognitive Sciences, 4* (1), 29–34.

Barrett, J. L. & Van Orman, B. (1996). The effects of image-use in worship on God concepts. *Journal of Psychology and Christianity, 15* (1), 38–45.

Bastide, D. (1980). Religious education and the trainee first school teacher. *British Journal of Religious Education, 3* (1), 5–12.

Bastide, D. (1992). *Good practice in primary religious education 4–11*. London: The Falmer Press.

Bates, D. (1992). Developing RE in topic-based approaches to learning. In D. Bastide (Ed.), *Good practice in religious education 4–11*. London and Washington DC: The Falmer Press.

Bauer, P. J., Larkina, M., Gúler, E. & Burch, M. (2019). Long-term autobiographical memory across middle childhood: Patterns, predictors, and implications for conceptualizations of childhood amnesia. *Memory*, 27(9), 1175–1193. https://doi.org/10.1080/09658211.2019.1615511

Bauer, P. J. & Wewerka, S. S. (1995). One- to two-year olds' recall of events: The more expressed, the more impressed. *Journal of Experimental Child Psychology, 59*, 475–496.

Bellchambers, E. (2011). Strategies and resources: Using the skills of the non-specialist. In C. Erricker, J. Lowndes & E. Bellchambers (Eds.), *Primary religious education – A new approach* (pp. 163–184). London: Routledge.

Blaylock, L. (2004). Six schools of thought in RE. *Resource, 27* (1), 13–16.

Bovet, P. (1928). *The child's religion*. London & Co.

Brunschvicg, L. (1949). *L'experience humaine et la causalité physique*. PUF (first published in 1922, Paris: Alcan).

Bucher, A. A. (1991). Understanding parables: A developmental analysis. *New Directions for Child Development, 52*, 101–105.

Burt, Sir C. (1971). Religious education. *The Journal of the Association of Educational Psychologists-News Letter, 2* (8), 3–10.

Cassidy, C. (2012). Questioning children. *Thinking: The Journal of Philosophy for Children, 20* (1–2), 62–68.

Coley, J. D. (2000). On the importance of doing comparative research: The case of folk biology. *Child Development, 71* (1), 82–90.

Commission on Religious Education – Final Report (CoRE) (2018). *Religion and worldviews: The way forward.*

Cooling, T. (2020). Worldview in religious education: Autobiographical reflections on The Commission on Religious Education in England final report. *British Journal of Religious Education.* doi:10.1080/01416200.2020.1764497.

Corrigan, R. & Denton, P. (1996). Causal understanding as a developmental primitive. *Developmental Review, 16*, 162–202.

Cox, E. (1983). *Problems and possibilities in religious education.* London: Hodder and Stoughton.

Davis, E. B., Moriarty, G. L. & Mauch, J. C. (2013). God images and God concepts: Definitions, development and dynamics. *Psychology of Religion and Spirituality, 5* (1), 51–60.

De Roos, S. A., Iedema, J. & Miedema, S. (2001). Young children's descriptions of God: Influences of parents' and teachers' God concepts and religious denomination of schools. *Journal of Beliefs & Values, 22* (1), 19–30.

Elkind, D. (1964). Piaget's semi-clinical interview and the study of spontaneous religion. *Journal for the Scientific Study of Religion, 4*, 40–47.

Elkind, D. (1966). The developmental psychology of religion. In A. H. Kidd & J. L. Rivoire (Eds.), *Perceptual development in children* (pp. 193–225). London: University of London Press.

Elman, J. L., Bates, E. A., Johnson, M. H., Karmiloff-Smith, A., Parisi, D. & Planket, K. (1996). *Rethinking innateness: A connectionist perspective on development.* Cambridge, MA: The MIT Press.

Emmet, D. (1966). *The nature of metaphysical thinking.* London, UK: Macmillan.

Erricker, C. (2011a). Why is RE important? In C. Erricker, J. Lowndes & E. Bellchambers (Eds.), *Primary religious education – A new approach* (pp. 6–21). London: Routledge.

Erricker, C. (2011b). Why conceptual enquiry? In C. Erricker, J. Lowndes & E. Bellchambers (Eds.), *Primary religious education – A new approach* (pp. 52–90). London: Routledge.

Erricker, C. (2011c). Holistic and creative learning. In C. Erricker, J. Lowndes & E. Bellchambers (Eds.), *Primary religious education – A new approach* (pp. 91–117). London: Routledge.

Erricker, C. & Bellchambers, E. (2011). What next for RE and the primary curriculum? In C. Erricker, J. Lowndes & E. Bellchambers (Eds.), *Primary religious education – A new approach* (pp. 185–208). London: Routledge.

Estes, D., Wellman, H. M. & Woolley, J. D. (1989). Children's understanding of mental phenomena. In H. W. Reese (Ed.), *Advances in child development and behavior* (Vol. 22, pp. 41–87). San Diego, CA: Academic Press.

Evans, E. M. (2001). Cognitive and contextual factors in the emergence of diverse belief systems: Creation versus evolution. *Cognitive Psychology*, *42*, 217–266.
Ezer, M. (1962). The effect of religion upon children's responses to questions involving physical causality. In J. F. Rosenblith & W. Allinsmith (Eds.), *The causes of behaviour: Readings in child development and educational psychology* (pp. 481–487). Boston: Allyn & Bacon.
Fontana, D. (1971). College students' concepts of God. *Learning for Living*, *10* (5), 22–23.
Fowler, J. (1986). Faith and the structure of meaning. In C. Dykstra & S. Parks (Eds.), *Faith development and Fowler* (pp. 15–42). Birmingham, AL: Religious Education Press.
Frady, K. (2019). Rendering theology with 2-year-old children: A Godly play and grounded theory combination. *International Journal of Children's Spirituality*, *24* (2), 183–201.
Gates, B. (1977). Religion in the child's own core curriculum. *Learning for Living*, 9–15.
Gauch, H. G. (2009a). Science, worldviews, and education. *Science & Education*, *18*, 667–695.
Gauch, H. G. (2009b). Responses and classifications regarding science and worldviews. *Science & Education*, *18*, 905–927.
Gelman, R. (1990). First principles organize attention to and learning about relevant data: Number and the animate-inanimate distinction as examples. *Cognitive Science*, *14*, 79–106.
Gelman, R. (2000). Domain specificity and variability in cognitive development. *Child Development*, *71* (4), 854–856.
Gelman, R. (2002). On animates and other worldly things. In N. L. Stein, P. J. Bauer & M. Rabinowitz (Eds.), *Representation, memory and development: Essays in honor of Jean Mandler* (pp. 75–87). London, UK: Lawrence Erlbaum Associates.
Gelman, R. & Baillargeon, R. (1983). A review of some Piagetian concepts. In P. H. Mussen (Ed.), *Handbook of child psychology* (Vol. III, pp. 167–230). New York: John Wiley & Sons.
Gelman, R., Spelke, E. S. & Meck, E. (1983). What pre-schoolers know about animate and inanimate objects. In D. Rogers & J. A. Sloboda (Eds.), *The acquisition of symbolic skills* (pp. 297–326). New York, NY: Plenum Publishing Corporation.
Gelman, S. A. (2004). Psychological essentialism in children. *Trends in Cognitive Sciences*, *8* (9), 404–409.
Gelman, S. A. & Kremer, S. E. (1991). Understanding natural cause: Children's explanations of how objects and their properties originate. *Child Development*, *62*, 396–414.
Gelman, S. A. & Opfer, J. E. (2002). Development of the animate-inanimate distinction. In U. Goswami (Ed.), *Blackwell handbook of childhood cognitive development* (pp. 151–166). Malden, MA: Blackwell Publishers.
Gelman, S. & Wellman, H. M. (1991). Insides and essences: Early understandings of the non-obvious. *Cognition*, *38*, 213–244.
Goldman, R. (1964). *Religious thinking from childhood to adolescence*. London: Routledge and Kegan Paul.

Goldman, R. (1965). *Readiness for religion*. London: Routledge and Kegan Paul.
Golinkoff, R. M., Harding, C. G., Carlson, V. & Sexton, M. E. (1984). The infant's perception of causal events: The distinction between animate and inanimate objects. In L. P. Lipsitt & C. Royce-Collier (Eds.), *Advances in infancy research* (Vol. 3, pp. 145–151). Norwood, NJ: Ablex Publishing Corporation.
Goswami, U. (1992). *Analogical reasoning in children*. Hove, UK: Lawrence Earlbaum Associates Ltd.
Goswami, U. (Ed.) (2002). *Blackwell handbook of childhood cognitive development*. Oxford: Blackwell Publishers.
Greer, J. E. (1972). The child's understanding of creation. *Educational Review*, *24*, 99–110.
Grimmitt, M. H. (Ed.) (2000). *Pedagogies of religious education: Case studies in the research and development of good pedagogic practice in RE*. Great Wakering: McCrimmon.
Grimmitt, M. H. (2008). Inside a religious education research project: The influence of theological and educational considerations on the treatment of religious content within a prescribed pedagogic framework. *Journal of Beliefs & Values*, *29* (3), 223–232.
Halliwell, J. (1991). Quantum cosmology and the creation of the universe. *Scientific American*, December, 76–85.
Hannam, P. & Biesta, G. (2019). Religious education, a matter of understanding? Reflections on the final report of the Commission on Religious Education. *Journal of Beliefs & Values*, *40* (1), 55–63.
Harms, E. (1944). The development of religious experience in children. *American Journal of Sociology*, *50*, 112–122.
Harris, P. L. & Koenig, M. (2006). Trust in testimony: How children learn about science and religion. *Child Development*, *77* (3), 505–524.
Hatano, G. & Inagaki, K. (1994). Young children's naïve theory of biology. *Cognition*, *50*, 171–188.
Hay, D. & Nye, R. (1996). Investigating children's spirituality: The need for a fruitful hypothesis. *The International Journal of Children's Spirituality*, *1* (1), 6–16.
Hay, D. & Nye, R. (1998). *The spirit of the child*. London: Fount.
Heland-Kurzak, K. A. (2019). Children's creation of an image of God and religiosity – a pedagogical perspective. *International Journal of Children's Spirituality*, *24* (4), 434–446.
Heller, D. (1985). The children's God. *Psychology Today*, December, 22–27.
Hill, P. C., Pargament, K. I., Hood, R. W., McCullough, M. E., Swyers, J. P., Larson, D. B. & Zinnbauer, B. J. (2000). Conceptualizing religion and spirituality: Points of commonality, points of departure. *Journal for the Theory of Social Behavior*, *30* (1), 51–77.
Hinde, R. A. (1999). *Why gods persist: A scientific approach to religion*. London: Routledge.
Howkins, K. G. (1966). *Religious thinking and religious education: A critique of the research and conclusions of Dr R.* Goldman. London: Tyndale Press.
Hull, J. (2000). Religion in the service of the child project: The gift approach to religious education. In M. Grimmitt (Ed.), *Pedagogies of religious education: Case*

studies in the research and development of good pedagogic practice in RE (pp. 112–129). Great Wakering: McCrimmon.

Jackson, R. (1990). Children as ethnographers. In R. Jackson & D. Starkings (Eds.), *The junior RE handbook*. Cheltenham, UK: Stanley Thornes (Publishers) Ltd.

Jackson, R. (2000). The Warwick religious education project: The interpretative approach to religious education. In M. Grimmitt (Ed.), *Pedagogies of religious education: Case studies in the research and development of good pedagogic practice in RE* (pp. 130–152). Great Wakening, UK: McGrimmon.

Jackson, R. & Starkings, D. (Eds.) (1990). *The junior RE handbook*. Cheltenham, UK: Stanley Thornes (Publishers) Ltd.

Kant, I. (1983). *The critique of pure reason*. London: The Macmillan Press.

Kay, W. K. (2002). Rethinking primary religious education. *Journal of Beliefs & Values, 23* (2), 203–216.

Keil, F. C. (1979). *Semantic and conceptual development: An ontological perspective*. Cambridge, MA: Harvard University Press.

Keil, F. C. (1981). Children's thinking: What never develops. *Cognition, 10*, 159–166.

Keil, F. C. (2006). Explanation and understanding. *Annual Review of Psychology, 57*, 227–254.

Kelemen, D. & DiYanni, C. (2005). Intuitions about origins: Purpose and intelligent design in children's reasoning about nature. *Journal of Cognition and Development, 6* (1), 3–31.

Kiessling, F. & Perner, J. (2014). God-mother-baby: What children think they know. *Child Development, 85* (4), 1601–1616.

Kikas, E. (1998). The impact of teaching on students' definitions and explanations of astronomical phenomena. *Learning and Instruction, 8* (5), 439–454.

Knight, G. P. & Zerr, A. A. (2007). Measurement equivalence in child development research. *Child Development Perspectives, 4* (1), 1–4.

Koenig, H. G. (2008). Concerns about measuring "spirituality" in research. *The Journal of Nervous and Mental Disease, 196* (5), 349–355.

Kohn, E. (2019). Designing a curriculum framework for school prayer: A case study from UK Jewish primary schools. *Religious Education, 114* (2), 155–167.

Kóksal-Tuncer, O. & Sodian, B. (2018). The development of scientific reasoning: Hypothesis testing and argumentation from evidence in young children. *Cognitive Development, 48*, 135–145.

Leddon, E. M., Waxman, S. R. & Medin, D. L. (2008). Unmasking "alive": Children's appreciation of a concept linking all living things. *Journal of Cognition and Development, 9* (4), 461–473.

Long, D., Elkind, D. & Spilka, B. (1967). The child's conception of prayer. *Journal for the Scientific Study of Religion, 6* (1), 101–109.

Lowndes, J. (2011a). What is good RE? In C. Erricker, J. Lowndes & E. Bellchambers (Eds.), *Primary religious education – A new approach* (pp. 22–33). Abingdon, UK: Routledge.

Lowndes, J. (2011b). Creating an enquiry-based curriculum. In C. Erricker, J. Lowndes & E. Bellchambers (Eds.), *Primary religious education – A new approach* (pp. 136–162). Abingdon, UK: Routledge.

McCreery, E. (2005). Preparing primary school teachers to teach religious education. *British Journal of Religious Education, 27* (3), 265–277.

McKelvie, J. (1996). *Children's reactions to being asked to draw God.* Unpublished manuscript. UK: University of Buckingham.

Madge, V. (1965). *Children in search of meaning.* London: SCM Press Ltd.

Making Sense of Religion (2007). Ofsted No. 070045. www.ofstead.gov.uk

Mandler, J. M. (1990). Recall and its verbal expression. In R. Fivush & J. A. Hudson (Eds.), *Knowing and remembering in young children* (pp. 317–330). New York: Cambridge University Press.

Mandler, J. M. (2004). Thought before language. *Trends in Cognitive Sciences, 8* (11), 508–513.

Mandler, J. M. & McDonough, L. (1993). Concept formation in infancy. *Cognitive Development, 8*, 291–318.

Margett, T. E. & Witherington, D. C. (2011). The nature of preschoolers' concepts of living and artificial objects. *Child Development, 82* (6), 2067–2082.

Massey, C. & Gelman, R. (1988). Preschoolers' ability to decide whether a photographed unfamiliar object can move itself. *Developmental Psychology, 24*, 307–317.

Matthews, G. (1984). *Dialogues with children.* Cambridge, MA & London, UK: Harvard University Press.

Medawar, P. (1984). *The limits of science.* New York, NY: Harper & Row.

Miller, J. & McKenna, U. (2011). Religion and religious education: Comparing and contrasting pupils' and teachers' views in an English school. *British Journal of Religious Education, 33* (2), 173–187.

Mitchell, B. (1980). Religious education. *Oxford Review of Education, 6* (2), 133–139.

Mountain, V. (2005). Prayer is a positive activity a report on recent research. *International Journal of Children's Spirituality, 10* (3), 291–305.

Nye, W. C. & Carlson, J. S. (1984). The development of the concept of God in children. *Journal of Genetic Psychology, 145*, 137–142.

Nye, R. & Hay, D. (1996). Identifying children's spirituality: How do you start without a starting point? *British Journal of Religious Education, 18* (3), 144–154.

Petrovich, O. (1988a). *An examination of Piaget's theory of childhood artificialism.* Unpublished D.Phil. thesis, University of Oxford.

Petrovich, O. (1988b). Re-review of Goldman's (1964) Religious thinking from childhood to adolescence (London: Routledge & K. Paul). *Modern Churchman, 30* (2), 44–49.

Petrovich, O. (1999). Preschool children's understanding of the dichotomy between the natural and the artificial. *Psychological Reports, 84*, 3–27.

Petrovich, O. (2019). *Natural-theological understanding from childhood to adulthood.* London and New York: Routledge.

Piaget, J. (1925). La representation du monde chez l'enfant. *Revue de Théologie et de Philosophie, 13*, 191–214.

Piaget, J. (1977). *The child's conception of the world.* Paladin.

Piaget, J. (1928). Immanence et transcendance. In J. Piaget & J. De La Harpe (Eds.), *Deux types d'attitudes religieuses: Immanence et transcendence* (pp. 7–40). Labor á Genéve: Editions de l'Association Chrétienne d'Etudiants de Suisse Romande.

Pitts, V. P. (1977). Drawing pictures of God. *Learning for Living, 16*, 123–129.

Pnevmatikos, D. (2002). Conceptual changes in religious concepts of elementary schoolchildren: The case of the house where God lives. *Educational Psychology, 22* (1), 93–112.

Polkinghorne, J. (2002). The credibility of the miraculous. *Zygon, 37* (3), 751–757.
Reiss, M. (2009). Imagining the world: The significance of religious worldviews for science education. *Science & Education, 18*, 783–796.
Revell, L. (2005). Student primary teachers and their experience of religious education in schools. *British Journal of Religious Education, 27* (3), 215–226.
Richards, D. D. & Siegler, R. S. (1986). Children's understanding of the attributes of life. *Journal of Experimental Child Psychology, 42*, 1–22.
Rymarz, R. & Belmonte, A. (2020). The questions students ask? A preliminary examination of the questions raised in religious education classes in Catholic schools. *British Journal of Religious Education, 42* (2), 120–128.
Schweitzer, F. (2005). Children's right to religion and spirituality: Legal, educational and practical perspectives. *British Journal of Religious Education, 27* (2), 103–113.
Shtulman, A., Foushee, R., Barner, D., Dunham, Y. & Srinivasan, M. (2019). When Allah meets Ganesha: Developing supernatural concepts in a religiously diverse society. *Cognitive Development, 52*, 100806. https://doi.org/10.1016/j.cogdev.2019.100806
Simons, D. J. & Keil, F. C. (1995). An abstract to concrete shift in the development of biological thought: The *insides* story. *Cognition, 56*, 129–163.
Sorea, D. & Scarneci-Domnisoru, F. (2018). Unorthodox depictions of divinity. Romanian children's drawings of Him, Her or It. *International Journal of Children's Spirituality, 23* (4), 380–400.
Spelke, E. S. (2000). Nativism, empiricism, and the origins of knowledge. In D. Muir & A. Slater (Eds.), *Infant development: The essential readings* (pp. 36–51). Oxford, UK: Blackwell.
Springer, K. & Keil, F. C. (1989). On the development of biologically specific beliefs: The case of inheritance. *Child Development, 60*, 637–648.
Stern, J. (2018). *Teaching RE: Researchers in the classroom.* Bloomsbury Academic.
Sully, J. (1903). *Studies of childhood.* London, UK: Longmans, Green & Co.
Takriti, R. A., Barrett, M. & Buchanan-Barrow, E. (2006). Children's understanding of religion: Interviews with Arab-Muslim, Asian-Muslim, Christian and Hindu children aged 5–11 years. *Mental Health, Religion & Culture, 9* (1), 29–42.
The Holy Bible: New International Version. (1980). London, UK: Hodder & Stoughton.
The National Secular Society Briefing Paper, September 2013. doi:https://www.secularism.org.uk/uploads/religious-education-briefing-paper.pdf
Van Der Kooij, J. C., De Ruyter, D. J. & Miedema, S. (2017). The merits of using "worldview" in religious education. *Religious Education, 112* (2), 172–184.
Vergote, A., Tamayo, A., Pasquilli, L., Bonami, M., Pattyn, M. & Custers, C. (1969). Concept of god and parental images. *Journal for the Scientific Study of Religion, 8* (1), 79–87.
Vosniadou, S. & Ortony, A. (1983). The emergence of the literal-metaphorical-anomalous distinction in young children. *Child Development, 54*, 154–161.
Waddup, H. (1992). Planning RE across an infant school. In D. Bastide (Ed.), *Good practice in religious education 4–11* (pp. 24–46). London: The Falmer Press.
Ward, K. (2002). Believing in miracles. *Zygon, 37* (3), 741–750.
Wellman, H. M. & Gelman, S. A. (1992). Cognitive development: Foundational theories of core domains. *Annual Review of Psychology, 43*, 337–375.

Wellman, H. M. & Gelman, S. A. (1998). Knowledge acquisition in foundational domains. In W. Damon, D. Kuhn & R. S. Siegler (Eds.), *Handbook of child psychology* (pp. 523–574).

Wenger, J. L. (2001). Children's theories of God: Explanations for difficult-to-explain phenomena. *The Journal of Genetic Psychology*, *162* (1), 41–55.

Zinnbauer, B. J., Pargament, K. & Scott, A. B. (1999). The emerging meanings of religiousness and spirituality: Problems and prospects. *Journal of Personality*, *67* (6), 889–919.

Author Index

Amsel, E. 8
Attfield, D. G. 4, 7, 107n1

Baillargeon, R. 5, 38, 71, 101
Barrett, J. L. 6, 95
Barrett, M. 91
Bastide, D. 2, 10, 35, 84, 86, 98
Bates, D. 96, 98
Bauer, P. J. 101, 103
Bellchambers, E. 2, 10, 106
Belmonte, A. 19, 74
Biesta, G. 13
Blaylock, L. 99
Bovet, P. 3–4, 6
Brunschvicg, L. 53
Bucher, A. A. 5
Burt, Sir C. 11, 99

Carlson, J. S. 5–6, 10, 75n2, 93
Carlson, V. 48
Cassidy, C. 70, 74
Coley, J. D. 67
Cooling, T. 13
Corrigan, R. 52
Cox, E. 4, 11, 99

Davis, E. B. 74n1
De Roos, S. A. 93
De Ruyter, D. J. 13
Denton, P. 52
DiYanni, C. 58

Elkind, D. 5–6, 30, 93
Elman, J. L. 101
Emmet, D. 41
Erricker, C. 2, 10, 89, 91, 94, 96, 106
Estes, D. 65, 100
Evans, E. M. 58
Ezer, M. 58

Fontana, D. 97, 99
Fowler, J. 4, 99
Frady, K. 100–1

Gates, B. 7
Gauch, H. G. 13
Gelman, R. 5, 9, 38, 48
Gelman, S. 5, 8, 38, 46, 48, 60, 77, 91, 93, 100
Goldman, R. 3–8, 74, 95, 98, 100
Golinkoff, R. M. 48
Goswami, U. 77, 98
Greer, J. E. 5
Grimmitt, M. H. 2, 10, 15, 35, 92

Halliwell, J. 53
Hannam, P. 13
Harding, C. G. 48
Harms, E. 7
Harris, P. L. 6
Hatano, G. 48
Hay, D. 12–13
Heland-Kurzak, K. A. 93
Heller, D. 4, 7
Hill, P. C. 12
Hinde, R. A. 4
Howkins, K. G. 7
Hull, J. 101

Iedema, J. 18–19, 93
Inagaki, K. 48

Jackson, R. 15, 92

Kant, I. 60, 74
Kay, W. 2, 10, 35, 101
Keil, F. C. 48, 58n1, 60, 67, 93
Kelemen, D. 58
Kiessling, F. 6
Kikas, E. 8, 91
Koenig, H. G. 12–13
Koenig, M. 6
Kohn, E. 2, 32, 83
Kremer, S. E. 46
Kóksal-Tuncer, O. 71

Leddon, E. M. 48
Long, D. 30
Lowndes, J. 2, 10, 92, 94–5, 101, 103

Madge, V. 70, 74, 75n3, 92
Mandler, J. M. 24, 38, 93, 100
Margett, T. E. 48
Massey, C. 48
Matthews, G. 105
Mauch, J. C. 74n1
McCreery, E. 2, 89, 102
McDonough, L. 38, 100
McKelvie, J. 7
McKenna, U. 18
Meck, E. 48
Medawar, P. 53
Medin, D. L. 48
Miedema, S. 13, 18–19, 93
Miller, J. 18
Mitchell, B. 103
Moriarty, G. L. 74n1
Mountain, V. 10, 74

Nye, R. 12–13
Nye, W. C. 5–6, 10, 75n2, 93

Opfer, J. E. 48
Ortony, A. 98

Pargament, K. 12
Perner, J. 6
Petrovich, O. 4, 6, 13, 15, 17, 39n5; & n6, 41–3, 45–9, 52, 56, 58n1, 59–60, 67, 89, 91, 95–6, 99, 101
Piaget, J. 3–10, 15, 53, 58, 85–6, 93
Pitts, V. P. 7
Pnevmatikos, D. 7
Polkinghorne, J. 5

Reiss, M. 13, 92
Revell, L. 2, 84, 89, 102
Richards, D. D. 48
Rymarz, R. 18–9, 74

Scarneci-Domnisoru, F. 91
Schweitzer, F. 1, 94
Scott, A. B. 12
Sexton, M. E. 48
Shtulman, A. 74
Siegler, R. S. 48
Simons, D. J. 48
Sodian, B. 71
Sorea, D. 91
Spelke, E. S. 38, 48, 71, 101
Spilka, B. 12, 30
Springer, K. 48
Starkings, D. 15
Stern, J. 15
Sully, J. 3, 53

Takriti, R. A. 91

Van Der Kooij, J. C. 13
Van Orman, B. 95
Vergote, A. 4
Vosniadou, S. 98

Waddup, H. 95, 101
Ward, K. 5
Waxman, S. R. 48
Wellman, H. M. 5, 8, 38, 60, 65, 77, 91, 93, 100
Wenger, J. L. 10–11, 35, 93
Wewerka, S. S. 101
Witherington, D. C. 48
Woolley, J. D. 65, 100

Zinnbauer, B. J. 12

Subject Index

agreed syllabus 101–2
Anglican; *see* school denominations
Animacy Task 42, 48–50
anthropomorphism 3, 6, 36–37, 72, 74
Artificial Derived/Artificial Primary condition 43–8
artificialism 3–4, 53

Bible 4–5, 7, 21, 34–6, 67–9, 74, 80, 87, 98, 100
Bible story box 100

Catholic; *see* school denominations
causal: criterion 41; inferences 59; judgements 58; mechanisms 17, 42–3, 46–7, 60; powers 68, 70, 82; principle 52, 56; reasoning 43, 53, 60, 71
causes: extrinsic 41, 46–7; intrinsic 45, 47, 60
childhood amnesia 103
child-adult comparisons 9, 67
children's abilities: abstract 3, 10–11; cognitive 5, 102; and interests 11, 61, 89–90, 92, 96, 101–3; speculating 53
Commission on Religious Education 1, 2, 11, 89
CoRE; *see* Commission on Religious Education
cosmological: conjectures 41, 54; hypotheses 53; judgements 54–6, 58; questions 42, 53–4, 58

Deen 21
denominational RE; *see* religious education
developmental psychology: contemporary 3, 6, 9, 15, 30, 37, 53, 86, 98, 102, 104–107; its research 3, 6, 8–10, 12, 15, 30, 91; Piagetian 5, 7, 9; teachers' knowledge of 11–12, 82, 85
dichotomies, ontological 41, 48, 52; animate-inanimate 41, 48; mental-physical 41; natural-artificial 41, 48

Evangelical; *see* school denominations

foundational: concepts 5, 59, 91, 93; RE; *see* religious education

God: concept(s) of 6–7, 10–12, 17, 19, 25, 32, 38, 43, 58, 60–1, 62–5, 77, 80, 86, 99, 100, 106; abstract 6–7, 10, 17–18, 36, 60–2, 65, 74, 77–80, 93, 99; as causal agent 43, 60, 91; as moral agent 69, 106; communication with 70; concrete 17, 60–4, 66, 73, 78–80, 82, 89; representations of 42, 60–2, 72–3, 95; unknowability 68; *see also* image justification; image of God; questions about God
Godly play 100

Hindu; *see* school denominations

image justification 61–4
image of God 60–64, 75n2, 80
innateness 101

Jewish; *see* school denominations

Kodesh 21

language: acquisition 8–9, 25, 28–9, 33, 45, 83–4, 93, 98, 114; development 6, 11–12, 15, 49–50, 65

matter: origin of; *see* cosmological judgements
memory: development of 101, 103; across life-span 101, 105; skills 24; test of 16, 21–2, 28, 36
multi-faith: pedagogy 11; primary RE 78, 80, 86, 88, 93, 102; society 2, 95; syllabus 1
Muslim; *see* school denominations
"My second sermon" painting 103–4, *104*

Natural Derived/Natural Primary condition 43–47
natural-theological reasoning test 16–18, 42–3, 54, 59, 89
non-faith; *see* school denominations

ontological, defined 58n1; knowledge 41, 43; *see* dichotomies
origin: antecedent-derived 17, 41–3, 45–7, 52; primary 17, 42, 45, 47, 50, 52, 59
Origin Task 42–48

parental religion 4, 6, 79
parental: expectations 95; preferences 98
PGCE training 11, 85, 95, 102
picture test; *see* natural-theological reasoning test
primary education 3, 9
primary RE: and developmental psychology 9–10, 89, 99–101; cognitive-developmental case for 3, 98–99; literature 2, 16, 74; purpose of 18, 78, 86–7, 92; requirements for 10

question(s) about God 16, 36, 38, 59, 61–2, 63–64, 67, 70–1, 82, 88, 90, 96, 106

RE; *see* religious education
RE interview: perceptions and attitudes to school RE 21–38; procedure 21–2; session 16
Religion and Worldviews Report 1
religious cognition 8, 10, 101, 105
religious concepts: acquired vs. spontaneous 5–6, 8, 59, 78
religious education: challenges 3, 11, 16, 96, 102; child-centred 94, 101; compulsory school subject 1, 103; and developmental research 8–12; denominational 105–107; developmental psychology 104–7; ethnographic research 15; foundational 105–7; framework of 2; implicit approach to 4; legal and social rights to 94; life themes approach 95; multi-faith conception of 93; psychology and 3–8; school assemblies 16, 21, 26, 30–2, 86; school-based 91, 94, 96–97; stories 16, 32, 35–6, 87–8, 95, 98, 102; syllabuses 101–2; teachers' perceptions and training 84, 89, 97–98
"religious foundations" 107n1
religious identity 19, 88
religious words 16, 21, 26–28, 83, 102

scientific: concepts 13; development 105; education 106–7; "ideas" 92; knowledge 49, 58, 99; reasoning 58; understanding 105
school denominations: Anglican 17, 23–5, 27, 30–3, 45, 50–1, 55, 57, 63–4, 72; Evangelical 17, 21, 23–5, 27, 30–1, 33, 45, 50–1, 55–7, 64; Catholic 17, 19, 23–5, 27, 30–3, 45, 50–1, 55–8, 64, 74, 85; Hindu 17, 21, 23, 25, 26–7, 30–1, 33, 45, 50–1, 55–7, 61, 63–4, 71–3, 81, 83–4, 88; Jewish 17, 21, 23–7, 30–3, 37, 45, 50–1, 55, 57–8, 63–4, 72–3, 81, 83–4, 88; Muslim 17, 21, 23–7, 30–1, 33, 37, 45, 50–1, 55, 57, 64, 72–3, 81, 83–4, 88; non-denominational (non-faith) 16–7, 22–3, 25, 27–8, 30–3, 39n1, 45, 50–1, 55–8, 63–4, 77; differences 22, 24, 30–1, 38, 50, 52, 54, 57, 78, 86; similarities 21, 38, 45, 52, 73, 78, 87
spirituality, definitions of 12–13; children's 85, 93

teacher-training: courses/programmes 3, 78, 84, 89–90, 98, 102

worldview(s) 1, 12–13

For Product Safety Concerns and Information please contact our EU representative GPSR@taylorandfrancis.com
Taylor & Francis Verlag GmbH, Kaufingerstraße 24, 80331 München, Germany

www.ingramcontent.com/pod-product-compliance
Ingram Content Group UK Ltd.
Pitfield, Milton Keynes, MK11 3LW, UK
UKHW020136200926
475702UK00005B/778